M. Stockley
March 1985

Voyage to Freedom

Voyage to Freedom

My Story of Hope

Phung Ngoc Sang

with

Frida Harris

Marshalls

Marshalls paperbacks
Marshall Morgan & Scott
3 Beggarwood Lane,
Basingstoke, Hants, RG23 7LP

First published by Marshall Morgan & Scott Ltd.

ISBN 0 551 01156 4

Typeset by Brian Robinson, North Marston, Bucks.

Printed in Great Britain by
Anchor Brendon Limited, Tiptree, Essex

Acknowledgements

Many people have been involved in the writing of this book and I would like to express my gratitude for the help so willingly given.

Particular thanks go to Dr GB Salmon MRCP of Southampton (Sang's GP), the General Hospital itself and Mr JL Munro FRCS for their help with medical terminology; the BRC (British Refugee Council); Lloyds Bank in New Milton and Lloyds Bank International (London); Southern Asian Outreach (Swindon); Dr Cameron Tallach (Peace Clinic, Hong Kong); Dr. Graham Fowler MRCGP (Staunton, Gloucester).

Thanks to Faber and Faber for granting permission to include quotations from Chinese poetry translated from the Chinese in Jonathan Spence's book: *The Gate of Heavenly Peace*.

I am grateful too for the co-operation of the Rev Roy Hicks of Hurn Christian Fellowship Church; to Richard Carr-Gomm for his preface about the Carr-Gomm Society Homes and to Mary Wang for her willing help over the Foreword; to Pat Pile and Mrs. Horsburgh for photographs and to my Chinese friend Nhi for her valued help on the Chinese scene in general and Chinese poetry in particular. Many of my close friends deserve my sincere thanks for their unfailing encouragement when the going was 'tough'.

My deepest gratitude goes to Rev Michael Meadows (OMF) for his untiring zeal and patience in the recording sessions and journeys to and from Southampton and to London.

The name *PHUNG NGOC SANG* is used throughout the book in place of Sang's actual name, by request; similarly, the names of his large family have been changed.

To Michael,
with gratitude for his invaluable
help in translating from Chinese.

Contents

Foreword

Throughout history, many have migrated from their own countries to another for various reasons. One of the tragedies in this century is that wars and rumours of wars have caused thousands to become homeless refugees.

Most of the host countries who have received the refugees for resettlement are countries with a Christian heritage. And this deed of mercy can be traced back to the law that God gave Moses for His people. '*Do not oppress an alien; you yourselves know how it feels to be aliens, because you were aliens in Egypt'* (Exodus 23.9), and '*When an alien lives with you in your land, do not ill-treat him. The alien living with you must be treated as one of your native-born. Love him as yourself, for you were aliens in Egypt. I am the Lord your God'* (Leviticus 19.33–34).

The message is clear when one's life, no matter how tragic and hopeless, is touched by God, there is hope, there is thankfulness, and both come from God.

Mary Wang
Director, Chinese Overseas Christian Mission.

Preface

Our society was founded to help those who are on their own. We have only been in existence for just over a decade and a half and we are learning all the time. With sixty small houses spread all over England, it has been possible for those living with us to play a part in the pioneering element of our work and to develop their own lives within it.

For that reason alone, the arrival and presence of Sang has been a joy and a revelation. He was our first boat resident - not speaking English, with no friend nor relation to speak for him and with neither possessions nor claim on official generosity.

He settled and he stayed. He smiled and asked for nothing. He seemed content but must have been in turmoil. His story in this book will tell you why.

But how and why was Sang a joy and a revelation? I must first tell you about our homes and you will understand. Each is different, yet each has the same ingredients - and these are mainly human. Admittedly, the building itself is one factor - whether it is a flat or a house, in the country or a tower block, an inner city area or a leafy suburb. The machinery or pattern of running its administration is also an ingredient.

But the main ingredients are the residents, the housekeepers, the neighbours and the community. It is only these people who can either overcome, or help to overcome, loneliness. It is their nature and personalities which make the difference - the reactions they have, the atmosphere they create, how much they share.

Each of our homes is filled with a group of mixed age and sex and with different reasons for coming, but all are single and agree to play a part in being one of a family or group. So mixed colours, religions and politics are the norm to us; we do not notice them.

Sang, though, was different – we only knew his background through general newspaper stories about the war in Vietnam; we could not communicate because we had no common language; his culture was unlike any we had met before. So to find that we could still help and be useful was both a joy and a revelation. It opened up new vistas for us, shook the whole society out of its parochialism and told us how much more work we could do beyond the confines of the ordinary, with which we were accustomed. That was joyful.

To learn that Sang was prepared to take us as we were, not to criticise but to accept, to be cheerful despite all that happened: that was a revelation. To see his faith grow and his Christianity conquer all his problems was something we needed, and need, to see time and time again. He tells his own story through Frida, who has inspired him (and us), and we are happy and grateful to be part of it.

Richard Carr-Gomm
(Founder and adviser of the
Carr-Gomm Society Homes for the Lonely)

INTRODUCTION

A visit to Phung Ngoc Sang

The idea for this book was born one day in 1983, when I was visiting my former student Phung Ngoc Sang in his Southampton home 'Bethany House', one of the Carr-Gomm Society homes for lonely men and women.

'Is your life here so very different from Vietnam', I asked Sang, as he entertained me and we chatted about the past.

'Oh yes, very different,' he replied. 'There I was living within a large family circle. There we were business people with plenty of money. We were rich and prosperous, at least until 1954 when the Communists took over our country. Things changed then.'

'You have security and freedom here,' I persisted, wanting to draw him out.

'Yes, but now I am a single person in a strange land. I have lost my wife, my son, my family and my money. I have been deserted.'

'I didn't know you were married,' I went on, hesitant to probe, yet with a sense that Sang wanted me to know. 'Where are your wife and your son now?'

And then Sang began to tell me his story – a story of desertion in his time of need, of his utter desolation, his loneliness; of the sufferings and frustrations that he and his family had suffered since the Communists took over Vietnam.

'Yet you look so happy,' I continued. 'Whenever I see you, you are smiling and contented.'

'I have someone to rely on now,' said Sang, with the radiant smile I had come to know so well. 'I can rely on the Lord, because now I know Him. In Vietnam I didn't know God at all – all my family were atheists. In Hong Kong I began to believe. But now I have a stronger faith in Jesus Christ. He has given me salvation. Now the Lord Jesus is even more precious to me than my parents, though of course I long to see them again. What I want most of all is the presence of the Lord. Before I became a Christian time used to hang heavy, but now there is not enough time to read the Bible and learn about the Lord. I thank God He is teaching me. He is giving me knowledge, but I am not worthy of His love. I don't come up to the standards of other Christians, but I love the Lord for ever. That I do know.'

As I listened to Sang then, I realised that in the past half-hour I had learnt more about him than in all the five months I had taught him English. Perhaps this was because *he* was now entertaining me. *He* was the host in his own home. Also there was no language problem, since we had a Chinese interpreter.

He went on to talk of his experiences in his early life in Vietnam, when his family was rich and prosperous; of his terrible job in the mountains working for the Communist Government after 1954; of the consequent breakdown of his health. He told me of the family decision to leave Vietnam, where the life had become impossible, and of the disastrous month-long voyage on the South China Seas.

'We even had a typhoon,' he said with a wry smile,'*and* our gold was all stolen, but when we reached Hong Kong . . .' He paused, his face again lighting up with a brilliant smile, '. . . that was the best of all for me.'

'Why?' I enquired. 'Most people found it very crowded and uncomfortable.'

'Yes, it was crowded and I was very ill while I was there, and we had bad news all the time. But it was at Hong Kong that I first heard the Good News of the

Gospel. After I had accepted Jesus as my Saviour, the other things did not seem so dreadful. Even though I had lost my health and lost my family I did not feel so desolate. I had a friend who would stand by me. And now in 1983 I can say He has stood by me all the way. And I am learning more about Him all the time.'

I had been privileged to teach Sang the rudiments of the English language for the five months he was based at Sopley Reception Centre in Hampshire. This was the camp that was opened up to receive the refugees who poured out of Vietnam in what became known as the Exodus of the Boat People. The camp was rough, it was crude, it was dreary, but it provided a haven for the destitute and a jumping-off ground to other parts of the United Kingdom. I worked there for three and a half years and many were the friendships made then and cemented later.

This one student, Sang, was special. He was a lone, weak, partially paralysed forty-year-old man in the midst of the huge extended families of the North and South Vietnamese; he had no family in England at all. He was a radiantly happy-looking man; he studied with more perseverance than all my other lovable, jovial students, yet until today I knew little of his background story. I knew he was an intelligent man, having had several years of education at Primary and Secondary level, followed by training as an interpreter between the Chinese and Vietnamese-speaking people.

My first introduction to Sang was in my Sopley classroom, as I set about the enthralling task of teaching the basics of our language. I noticed his completely paralysed right arm, hanging loosely at his side, the limping walk, but most of all the brilliance of his smile. I noticed the persistence in learning, the extra work studied in his hut, the determined way he attempted to write with his left hand, a skill he obviously found difficult.

One day, after the English lesson, Sang stopped me in

the corridor and asked, 'Teacher Frida, are you Christian?'

Because we had not 'done' the formation of simple questions, I rejected the evidence of my hearing, but on repetition, I realised that Sang had really wanted to know the answer to his question. He wanted to know if I was one of the same family as he was. As for me, I was so thrilled that I clutched him and almost knocked him over – he was very weak! This was a red-letter day for me too, as Sang was the first student ever to ask this question. I rejoiced as I told him he was my brother in the Lord. He didn't quite understand that but there was no disguising the joy he felt in having some family in a strange land.

As I sat with him in his own home that day, being entertained by him, I realised that Sang must have a story to tell. I had not heard anything of his life in Vietnam, of his family and the details of his illness. I had heard little of his job in the mountains or his visit to Peking, nor of the whole month he and his family had spent in a tiny boat on the open sea. Nor had I any idea that he and his family had been atheists. I could tell that what Sang most wanted to talk about was his conversion from atheism to Christianity. This was a greater change for him even than the change of country and culture.

'Would you let me write your story, from the time when you were living in Vietnam until now?' I asked Sang.

I spoke a little hesitantly. After all, many of the Vietnamese are very shy and resent any intrusion into their privacy. But Sang hardly allowed me to finish the sentence.

'Oh yes,' he assented heartily, 'but I would like to write it myself.'

And in a way, this is what we have done. It has been a compromise, for Sang's English is still elementary and my Chinese is non-existent, but with the help of a Christian translator, who speaks fluent Chinese and understands all the nuances of the intricate language, both written and spoken, the task has been done. Because the conversations and questions were all taped at the time, and because Sang spoke freely in his own language, much of his simple and sincere style has been preserved. It is *his* story. He wanted to tell it.

When I think back over the history of Sang's country, I realise how such stories as his have emerged from the chaos of years of war and instability.

To most of us, Vietnam is a country of which we only really became conscious during the '60s and '70s, when the United States became involved in the civil war between the Communist North and the Diem régime in the South. But the history of war and unrest in Vietnam goes back much further.

Vietnam has always existed uneasily in the shadow of China, but in the late 19th century it was France who colonised the country, and it was in resistance to French domination that the Communists began to organise in this century. Then, in the Second World War, the Japanese entered Vietnam, using it as a base against the allies. Ho Chi-minh then emerged as leader of the Communist troops who were organised to resist both French and Japanese. Japan collapsed in 1945, but from 1946 to 1954 war raged between the French and Ho Chi-minh's forces.

In 1954, when Ho Chi-minh had defeated the French, an agreement was signed, which partitioned the country and paved the way for civil war. Ho Chi-minh's Communist régime was established in the North, centred on Hanoi, and the Roman Catholic nationalist Ngo Dinh Diem had his régime in the South, centred on Saigon.

From that time, the country was in perpetual conflict. Sang describes, in his story how the Communist régime in the North brought very unwelcome changes to the lives of ordinary people there. And in South Vietnam, the Diem régime was equally tyrannical. By 1960 the Communist guerillas in the South, the Vietcong, had established a National Liberation Front and began to wage civil war, backed by the North.

In 1963 further conflict arose in the South between the Diem government and the majority Buddhist population, who were being persecuted by the régime. The Buddhists rioted, a military coup overthrew Diem, and he was assassinated. The next year the United States, who had supported Diem, stepped up their military intervention and bombed North Vietnam for the first time.

Between 1965 and 1973 seven million tons of bombs were dropped on Vietnam - that is three and a half times the entire Second World War total.

In 1975 the South Vietnamese government surrendered and the following year the country was united as the Socialist Republic of Vietnam. But peace did not make life more tolerable for families like Sang's in North Vietnam. On the contrary, they realised that the policies of the new government would make the future impossible for them.

Conflicts which arose between the new Vietnamese régime and China made the situation even worse for the many Vietnamese families of Chinese origin, and in the late '70s thousands were virtually expelled from the country. About 70 per cent of the Vietnamese refugees who came to Britain were ethnic Chinese people from North Vietnam.

Sang's story tells us something of the way families like his were affected by the Communist rule: how they were forced to give up their privately owned businesses; how university students were made to give up their studies and do manual work; how strict regulations and threats of reprisals for any breach of them created an atmosphere of fear and distrust; how the people came to dread being sent to the New Economic Zones – the rough forest lands that became the Vietnamese equivalent of Siberia.

The conflicts of ideologies involved are not really important. Thousands of ordinary Vietnamese people suffered immensely from the tyrannies of repressive government rule, both in the North and the South; from the actual war itself, and from the stringencies of post-war government regulations, without having much idea of the political implications behind the disruption of their lives. They knew only that they longed for genuine peace and freedom.

Out of the suffering and the tyranny a fierce determination has emerged. Out of their traumatic and often terrifying experiences a hope has evolved which has been like a life-line to the Vietnamese refugees. They must hold on to it, for it is sometimes all they have left. Without a hope within, a refugee has nothing – he is a dispossessed person, just another name on a list, just another number in the statistics.

For me, to listen to a story of endurance, determination and above all hope, has been a broadening experience: Sang has enriched my life. His material riches may have been taken from him but he remains rich in faith and hope; his physical weakness is compensated for by great spiritual strength. I pray that his story may inspire others and in particular that the hope that became an 'eternal spring' in him may be passed on to his readers.

SANG'S STORY

1: Early days in Vietnam

'Stop fiddling!' shouted my grandfather angrily.

My youngest brother Thanh always fiddled with everything he could lay his hands on: the radio, our bicycles, and anything electrical, but this time my grandfather was really cross. Thanh had been left alone in the medicine shop for just one minute and he had opened the drawers and mixed up all the powders.

We boys used to love watching the customers coming and going in this shop. Grandfather was regarded as a very important man in Nam Dinh, the small town about fifty miles from Hanoi in North Vietnam, where I was born. I loved my grandfather, though I was a little afraid of him. He had a long beard and very thick black hair that stood up on end. He was kind to us boys but strict. As a child I thought he was very, very old. I *knew* he was clever.

All along the walls behind the counter in the shop there were wooden panels. On these were written Chinese testimonials certifying what a good medicine man my grandfather was. As soon as I learned to read Chinese characters and was able to decipher these testimonials, I felt proud to be his grandson. I think I was his favourite grandchild, because I was so strong and healthy.

'You have a good body,' he used to say. 'You will never need my medicine. Keep strong! Live long!'

When I was small I used to think my grandfather would be glad if I were ill, so that he could make me better, but he had plenty of work with the really ill people. I often wondered if I would have a medicine shop myself one day.

I was fascinated by the medicine shop. Behind the counter there were many drawers. As a little boy of about five years old, I thought there were hundreds. None of them had names or numbers; my grandfather knew the contents by heart. To me, it seemed like magic! He would stand behind the counter and a woman would come in, bringing a prescription from the doctor. Grandfather would take the prescription, turn round quickly and, without looking, take seeds from one drawer, powders from another, herbs and grasses from a third and dried insects or lizards from a fourth. Some of the insects would be like little cockroaches. Then my grandfather would pull out a few hairs from his head or beard and put those too into the white paper, which he would then place on the scales. This was very important because the doctor prescribed all the medicines by weight. They would be wrapped up in a square packet and labelled.

That was not the end if the medicine was for children. Grandfather would go to different drawers and pick out some pickled or dried fruits, olives or oranges and he would put these in the paper too. This was for the children to eat after the medicine, if it was very bitter. They would pretend the medicine was bitter even if it wasn't, as they loved the sweet fruits so much! The ingredients had to be boiled up and the patients drank the juice only. Grandfather's medicines always made people better quickly. They trusted him.

When I was a small boy, I had a lot to do with shops because my parents had a dry-goods store just outside the town. We had plenty of money and two houses, because my father had always worked very hard. We were never short of anything. We children enjoyed seeing people come in to the shop, which they did at all hours of the day. The shop never seemed to shut. The people didn't only come to buy; they stopped to chat.

They showed off their babies and told all their news.

I was a happy little boy and very carefree. I did not worry about anything; there was nothing to worry about. I loved my family, my brothers and sisters. I came third in my family; I was born in 1940. Beside me, there were three more boys and three girls. We had plenty of aunts and uncles too, and our house was always full.

Education was quite important to us in North Vietnam. In every town and village there was a Primary School and about 32 per cent of the population attended full or part-time. I went to the school in Nam Dinh for six years. We called that school 'Small Learning' and I enjoyed it. I was strong and healthy and good at sports and games: I was the best runner in the whole school. I liked learning languages too and found it quite easy to learn Mandarin and Vietnamese; my own dialect was Cantonese. My language teachers were proud of me. But still I liked football, ping-pong and badminton best of all.

As I grew older, my parents bought me first a bicycle, then later, a motor-bike. This was great fun and my friends and I used to roar around the countryside. Sometimes we would ride out to the rivers and fish.

'Come on, you two boys,' my mother would call out to my friend Vinh and me as we cleaned up our bikes. 'We need some fish for the meal tonight. Fetch us some soles.'

There were plenty of soles in the rivers and Vinh and I were good at fishing. We used to sell some of our catch in the market. We were fond of shellfish too, and we used to have good prawn soup. And there was always plenty of rice, at least I can never remember going without. But Mama and Papa and my brother Hung remembered the year of the Great Famine. I was only a small boy of five at the time. The Famine wasn't caused by the Red River flooding. That happened every few years or so, but this was quite different.

'It was the Japanese,' Mama told us children. 'In 1940, as soon as they had invaded Vietnam, they refused to let us plant enough rice for the country. We had to plant jute.'

'Jute? What was jute for? You can't eat jute!'

'Jute was used for gunpowder,' she replied grimly. 'Japan needed a great deal of gunpowder and *we* had to supply it. So our own people died of starvation. There was not enough rice. That year, at least a million Vietnamese people died, while *they* made shells with our products!'

'But we are all alive,' I persisted. 'How did we get enough food?'

'We were better off in the towns,' Mama went on. 'Hanoi and Nam Dinh had good stores in the granaries. But many of the country people died.'

The Red River was a mixed blessing to the North Vietnamese. Hundreds of people lived in boats on the banks and on the river itself. The boats were sail-boats, sometimes with motors as well. They were about thirty to forty feet long and fishermen found them very convenient. If they needed to move to another area, it was a simple matter to take to the water and sail to a new site. They made a good living, as fishing was the second most important industry in Vietnam after rice.

But every four or five years, during the monsoon, the Red River burst its banks and there was excessive flooding. Hundreds of people suffered then. Many of the wooden houses were destroyed and if there were typhoons as well, trees were uprooted, all the electric wires blew down and there were many deaths.

I could remember this happening while I was still at Nam Dinh Primary School, but I did not feel any sorrow for the drowning people at that time. I was full of anger that the Government wouldn't do anything about it.

'It's stupid, Papa,' I raged. 'They know it's going to keep on happening. Why don't they do something about it?'

'The River gets all silted; all choked up,' he replied. 'It should be dredged. The same problem happens in China, I believe, when the Yellow River bursts its banks, but there they have managed to combat it. We haven't the mechanism to do the dredging here.'

'Why not?' I persisted. 'The Government should do something. That's what they're for, isn't it?'

I hated history and if it had not been for my brother Hung trying to explain it to me, I should have been ignorant of who was in charge of Hanoi. Apparently the Chinese and French had made an agreement in 1945. The Chinese had withdrawn leaving us a French colony, but with Ho Chi-minh, the nationalist leader, in effective control of North Vietnam.

'What's the matter with Ho Chi-minh?' I went on. 'He's the one who should do something, isn't he, Hung?'

'Yes,' Hung agreed, 'but he refuses to admit that the waters could penetrate into Hanoi. He doesn't want to admit it. He thinks it would be better for the waters to break their banks in another province so that other people would die.'

That made me even more angry.

'That's a strange way of coping with a problem,' I said.

'It's a very cruel way,' said my mother. 'What about our friends in Haiphong?' (Most of the people in Haiphong live on the river banks.)

'Why don't they leave their boat-homes and come and live in the city?' I asked.

'Fishing is their livelihood,' my father reminded me. 'You wouldn't want us to leave our shop, or Grandfather his medicine shop, would you?'

'No, we have a good life here,' I said. Although we were still a colony under the rule of the French and with Ho Chi-minh in real control, life in North Vietnam was pleasant on the whole. We had festivals through the year and we children used to look forward to these.

On the fifteenth of every eighth month there was a

special mid-Autumn festival for the children. All of us had huge lanterns in the shape of lions and we dressed in our best and had feasts. The lanterns were all lit and it was very bright and colourful.

On the fifteenth day of the seventh month, according to the country calendar as we called it, there was another sort of festival. I could never understand what it was all about, but we killed chickens and ducks and we worshipped the spirits. On this one day there was said to be forgiveness of sins for all those who were already in Hell. We kept the festival as a holiday, although my family were not keen Buddhists. The only religious ceremony that was important to us at home was the worshipping of our ancestors.

Sometimes we watched plays in the open-air cinemas and theatres, but they were almost always historical legends of old Chinese or Vietnamese history. I much preferred sport.

As I grew older, I became more interested in the old tales and customs. My favourite one was the story of the Lake of the Returned Sword. This was an actual lake in the middle of the city of Hanoi. It was called the Waan Kim Lake. An ancient king in Vietnamese history received a sword from the gods and with it he began to fight and conquer his enemies. When he returned to Hanoi, victorious over his enemies, he paid his respects to the sword, which to him included worshipping it, then he returned it to the lake from where it had come.

Ever since then on the first day of the fifth month, that is, International Labour Day, the festival of Waan Kim Lake is kept. It is also held on the second day of every ninth month, which is the National Day of Vietnam, and most important of all, it is kept on the last day of the old year. So these are three important holiday dates for us. On these days there are exhibitions of instrumental music and singing around the lake. There is no competition. It is done just for pleasure, in memory of the ancient king and his victories.

On the seventh day of the New Year it is everybody's birthday! There are lion and dragon dances and everyone is gay and happy.

Of course our Chinese New Year was the most important holiday of the whole year and it went on for many days. All the houses and the streets were brightly decorated, there were lion and dragon dances, we had fireworks and balloons. There were visits to all our friends and neighbours and the girls and women had smart new dresses. Mama was always very busy before the New Year, doing her special sewing and embroidery. My sisters were quite expert too. They used very fine silk, which came from the silk worms that were prolific in North Vietnam. There were thousands of acres of mulberry trees, on which the silkworms fed.

Our Vietnamese trees blossomed throughout all the seasons but mostly in the Spring. We were different from South Vietnam, which only had two seasons, the wet and the dry; we had four and although we were in the tropics, some of our nights were quite cold. We grew plums and cherries and many different kinds of oranges. We had green oranges with thin peel as well as huge orange coloured ones that were all very sweet and juicy.

There was no Middle School in Nam Dinh, so I had to go to Hanoi when I was twelve, and be a boarder at a large school there. We called it 'Middle Learning'. It was for children from twelve to eighteen years old. There were about 1,000 pupils and it was co-educational, which was quite unusual for North Vietnam. The next stage was the University, where my brother Hung was already studying. We used to call it 'Big Learning'. Not many reached that stage, but I hoped to do so.

At Middle School I learnt French. I was always happy when learning languages and new words, just like my younger sister Thu Thuy, but she turned everything into poetry. I did not like her poems very much, but I thought it very clever of her to write them. She was always reading old Chinese poetry too, and saying it aloud to me. It was a strange coincidence that my parents had named her Thu Thuy, meaning 'Autumn Water', a pure writer of beautiful words. Of course they had no idea that she would live up to her name.

As we grew older, Thu Thuy and I had more in common, though I still thought of life as revolving round fun and football.

Thu Thuy used to say, '*life* is a poem,' but I could not agree with her there. She had always found pleasure in beautiful things, just as my brother Thanh enjoyed mechanical and electrical things, and Hung was fascinated by history and the heritage of China. My older sister Ha Anh simply wanted to get married quickly and have lots of children; even when very young she was like a little mother to us boys. We laughed at her but we liked it! When my mother was busy in the shop, it was good to have Ha Anh make us nice things to eat; her cooking was excellent. When she married and went to live in Hong Kong, we all missed her very much.

We used to take turns when we were at home helping to watch the shop. Because it was open most of the day and right into the night and could never be left unattended, we children had to play our part. I enjoyed this, even as I grew older, but Hung hated it. He used to say, 'Oh Papa, I have more important things to do.' My father used to be cross about this, but secretly I think he was proud of his eldest son, who was getting on so well at Hanoi University.

'OK, but remember our money and success comes from hard work!' he told Hung, who nodded and went off to read about Confucius.

'But Confucius died so long ago,' I used to say to Hung. 'Life is going on now. . .*real* life, all round us! I am interested in the people of today.'

'Confucius died in 479 BC' Hung informed me. (He

never lost the chance of teaching us the things he learnt.) 'But the whole point of the works of Confucius was not only a record of history. His writings pointed morals; they mirror the times he lived in and show us how to correct our mistakes.'

'Better to make no mistakes in the first place,' remarked Thanh, laughing, as he worked patiently on the intricate parts of our alarm clock. 'I can't afford to make any mistakes when I work on an engine or a piece of electrical equipment. It would be too late to read about avoiding mistakes after I've been electrocuted!'

It was quite true. Thanh seldom made mistakes. I thought he was just as clever as Hung, but in a more practical way. And Thu Thuy with her poetry! I wasn't quite sure yet what my own special ability was to be, but I enjoyed school lessons and sport and I was interested in people. It was fun watching the people come into the shop and decide what they wanted to buy, and chatting to them. They never seemed to be in a hurry although they were always busy.

As I grew older, I noticed that the conversation in the shop appeared to be more serious. Sometimes the adults lowered their voices. This made the girls curious. They didn't like being left out of anything, but if anything was solemn, I preferred to avoid it. I would turn my thoughts to the next football match or plan a trip with my friend Vinh on our bikes. Life was not a poem to me, but it was very good.

'They keep whispering together, Sang,' Thu Thuy said to me. 'I don't like it. We never have secrets from each other.'

I shrugged my shoulders. 'Oh, don't worry yourself!' I said, 'it's grown-up talk. Why should you care? Everything is OK here.'

'But they *look* serious,' she persisted, 'and Mama's face is all lined. She sits quietly in the corner all day. She never laughs now.'

It was true. Even I had noticed that, but I thought she

was just growing older. But Mama was a happy woman and there had always been laughter and chattering in our house. The neighbours used our shop as a place to gossip. It had always been a noisy jolly place.

'Hung notices it too,' Thu Thuy went on. She could never leave a thing alone. She was like a dog worrying a bone. 'He says it's to do with the Government.'

I laughed at her. Thu Thuy seemed far too young to be bothering about Governments.

'Well, if it's the Government,' I said, still laughing, 'there's nothing *you* can do about it, so forget about it! Come out with Vinh and me!'

'No,' she pouted, 'I'm not a child to be put off with sweetmeats. You go off with your careless friends! Leave me to my thoughts.'

So I went off. Sometimes I didn't understand my little sister. I felt she was growing up much faster than I was and I felt left behind. And anyway, I hadn't offered her any sweetmeats!

'Governments!' I grumbled as Vinh and I took out our bikes and started off for an afternoon's pleasure. 'Who wants Governments?'

'What are you on about?' enquired Vinh. 'We have to have a Government. Where would we be without one?'

'Just here!' I retorted,'where we are now! It's not likely that the Government could have anything to do with our everyday lives!'

As I said before, I was extremely careless and carefree. Time and circumstances would very soon alter that!

2: Work; Illness; Peking

My school days were very happy. I had thoroughly enjoyed being one of the 100 boarders at Hanoi Middle School and had no wish to give up being 'one of the boys'. In my physical strength and mental ability, life had been good to me and the cares that had bowed my grandparents and parents had so far passed me by.

'It is time the boy grew up,' my father would say, seeing my excitement over football or a game of ping-pong. 'Life is not all fun.'

'But I like learning too,' I replied, for I was proud of my successes in learning languages. I had mastered the French language with no trouble at all and my teachers felt I should become an interpreter. I was looking forward to going to the University, like my brother Hung.

But in 1954 the French were defeated and left Vietnam, and Ho Chi-minh's Communist régime was established in the North of the country. Gradually our life in North Vietnam became different. The change was so gradual that at first we hardly noticed. But then, if we did anything that displeased the Government, our food rations were cut. We began to know hunger. Then the State began to take over business and industry, and private ownership was outlawed. When the authorities discovered that Hung was at University and that my parents were quite wealthy shop-owners, things changed rapidly. Hung was forced to leave the University. Under the new régime, the study of Chinese history was an irrelevant luxury, and educated people were a threat to the Government.

'It is too bad,' Hung complained. 'Now I shall never get a decent job.'

He was right. Almost at once he was forced to do manual labour. 'What is the use of a good brain, if I don't use it?' he asked. He became very bitter and was always brooding about what he could do about his life. But there was nothing he *could* do.

A sad day was dawning for my grandfather too. His shop had been his life and it had meant life for many people in Nam Dinh. In 1955 he was forced to give it up, and that same year he died. The completeness of our large family was broken and I was never the same carefree boy again. I was growing up and the future became more important to me.

At first, it did not seem so bad to me that my parents did not own their shop any more, because they still went on working in it, but change came here too. Very soon they were simply doing manual labour. My father was an excellent painter as well as a salesman, and the Communists discovered his talents. Father wrote and painted beautiful Chinese characters, and they made him print the labels for the new Eastern and Western medicines that were coming into Vietnam.

The Communists discovered my talents too and the Government soon found work for me. 'We have a good job for you,' they said. 'You will do useful work for the Government and use your talents at the same time.'

I thought it would be something like my father having to paint labels for the medicines, so at first I was not very interested, but when I heard what the work was, I felt very excited. I had always enjoyed adventure and my new job as an interpreter in mountainous country sounded like fun to me, although the pay did not sound very high.

'You will be working with a small team of seven or eight,' the Government official told me. 'The engineers are making maps for the Vietnamese Government and they will need translations from Chinese to Vietnamese.

It is a very important job. Your teachers from Hanoi tell us that you are a good translator.'

'Thank you,' I replied. 'That sounds the right sort of job for me. Where will the work be?'

'The work is in the mountains on the borders of China and Vietnam. It will be hard, tough work but you are a very strong young man. Your food will be provided for you. All you have to do is to keep up with the map-makers and translate for them.'

'OK, that sounds good,' I said, and I really believed it. Interpreting was my favourite occupation and the idea of working in the mountains did not deter me at all.

It was in May 1960 that I eventually set off for my first job. I felt sorry for Hung and my family, left behind to do the manual jobs that the Government had imposed on them, but for myself, my heart beat high with expectation.

I realised that I was now one of a huge organisation; there were about 2,000 of us divided into small teams and we had to cover all the large mountainous area between the two countries. Our first mountain was over 140 metres high. When the winter came there would be snow, although to begin with the weather was all right. But it was not very long before I understood what the official had meant by saying that the work was tough.

Some days we worked for ten hours, climbing up the sides of steep mountains, wading through rivers up to our necks, pushing our way through the deep forests and always feeling hungry. We worked so hard that we were hungry most of the time. Our food was very simple and inadequate and often the supplies broke down altogether. At one time, we were without food for a whole week. I think I could have coped with the hard work if we could have had enough to eat, but none of us felt really strong without food.

We had all taken anti-malaria tablets, so we thought we should be safe from forest illnesses, and we all wore strong boots because the place was infested with poisonous snakes. At night we slept in tents; one of us had to be on guard to warn us of enemies. Our chief enemies were bandits and wild animals. This is why we were provided with rifles, for the mountains were riddled with tigers, jackals and wild oxen. Even knowing that one of the team was on guard, we never felt completely free from fear,for sometimes the exhausted guard fell asleep or a silent jackal would creep up behind our tent.

We had the means to protect ourselves from bandits and wild animals, but nothing could keep us from the blood-sucking yellow flies and leeches that surrounded us, as well as the mosquitoes. Some mornings when we awoke our legs were covered with leeches.

'Why did they call this a good job?' I groaned one day, when I felt there was not an inch of my body that had not been bitten. 'Is it all as bad as this?'

There was an engineering expert from China in our team. He answered me. 'No,' he said, 'it's not all as bad as this area. This is the worst of the lot. That's why you and I are in this team.'

I was puzzled. 'Why?' I asked. It didn't seem fair.

'I'm in this team because I have the most experience and you are in it because you were the strongest interpreter available. Anyone with a health problem would not survive in this situation.'

Never before had I wished I had been able to claim a health problem! I began to have my first doubts as to whether I would be able to survive.

Altogether, with a few breaks between, I worked in those dangerous swampy, infested mountains and jungles for five years. My health gradually deteriorated, as did the health of the engineers. The rough eating and sleeping out in all weathers, the tough climbing and the dangers eventually took their toll and I was sent back to Nam Dinh

The doctor treated me, but I didn't get better. Eventually he said to me, 'There is no hope for you. You will die.'

I had some disease of the kidneys. They were not functioning properly. The doctor gave me two months to live, but I didn't lose heart. I told him I would discharge myself and I went to find a private doctor. He was more like my grandfather and he understood my illness.

He had a secret remedy handed down from former generations. With this special Chinese medicine,he said, my disease could be healed. I went to live in the doctor's house, paying my way. When two months had passed and I was still alive I felt hopeful. I went on with this medicine for about a year but its effect was very spasmodic. Sometimes I would feel quite better, sometimes worse. There was progress, but it was not consistent.

I have not mentioned my wife all this time. I had married in 1963 and we had one son, but as soon as I became ill, my wife was not good to me. She could not take the responsibility of having an ill husband, so my family had to look after me. I had nothing against my wife . . . no suspicions of infidelity, but although I put all my efforts into it, our marriage was hopeless. Eventually, in 1966, we were divorced and my son went with his mother. I was very much affected. I felt I had been deserted by them just when I needed them most.

My illness grew worse, so I put in an application to go to Peking, in the hope of finding complete healing. There was a better supply of medicine in China and I had an older sister there too, with whom I could stay when I was not having treatment. She lived in Tientsin, not too far away from Peking.

My sister's name was Xuan Linh. Her name represented the Spring season of the year, just as Thu Thuy's name represented Autumn.

'I don't know one single thing about Tientsin,' I told Thu Thuy as I made my preparations for the journey.

'It must be nice there,' she replied optimistically.

'Why?' I wanted to know. 'Xuan Linh has told us

very little of the place, only about her husband and children.'

'Of course,' agreed Thu Thuy. 'They are the most important things in her life, but Tientsin is very famous for its carpet making. Xuan Linh did tell us about that. Doesn't she work in a carpet factory herself?' I couldn't remember hearing anything about carpets. I suppose I was not really interested in them.

'And I know they grow delicious pears there,' went on my cheerful sister, 'and you must have heard the lines about Tientsin by the great poet Li Po.'

'Oh, no poetry now!' I begged, but she went on as usual:

> Tientsin in March
> Peach and plum blossom
> at every gate.

'We have plenty of blossoms here,' I said, 'and anyway, it's not March.'

But Thu Thuy laughed at me and repeated, 'I know you will like it there.'

'But this is 1966 and the Cultural Revolution is on. It will be very different today,' I argued.

'I hope not. Have faith!' said my sister.

'Yes, I have faith . . . faith that I will be healed in Peking,' I answered.

When I reached Tientsin, I saw no peach or plum blossom, because I had other things to think about. My interest was in the hospital.

This was the time when the Cultural Revolution in China had begun in earnest. Its appeal was particularly to youth, and the Communist Government, under Mao Tse-tung, had organised the young people into the Red Guards. These young people were fanatically devoted to Mao and, at that time, they were pouring into Peking from all parts of the country, in the hope of seeing their hero. Wearing their distinctive red armbands and carrying their little red books of Chairman Mao's writings, they milled about the city, so that in some places there was hardly room to walk. Some of them were very young - barely teenagers, and were very wild. They interpreted Mao's attacks on bourgeois culture as a licence to vandalise, and they destroyed many ancient monuments and valuable museum exhibits in their fervour.

I found the city totally chaotic and confusing, and I began to wish that I had stayed in Vietnam. I was afraid of what the outcome of my visit might be. However, I found the Ministry of Overseas Chinese and they listened to my story kindly enough. I told them about my long sickness resulting from the work I had done in the mountains, and the lack of medical supplies in Vietnam.

'We will give you a letter of introduction to the Yee Woh Hospital,' they said.'It is a large well-equipped hospital and they will be able to help you.'

Xuan Linh had told me about Yee Woh. It was so huge that to see the whole of it would take a day's visit. There were hills and boating lakes and several restaurants there. In the grounds there was a large museum, exhibiting artefacts from 1500 to 2000 years old; there were golden bowls, teacups, brass mirrors, shoes and old ships worked by paddles. These ships had been given to China by the Japanese.

'I should like to see that place,' I had said to my sister, some time before. But I had not expected to go as a patient.

I was a patient in that hospital for three months. I was very weak and my body was swollen. The doctors explained my condition to me, and I understood what had happened to me, but Chinese medical terms are not easy to translate into English. The Chinese believe that the body is an organic unity and our illnesses are caused by imbalance between the different organs. The cure is to restore the balance and harmony of the body. So the doctors in the Yee Woh Hospital would not only treat my kidneys, which were abnormal, but would try to find the cause. My blood pressure was too high also. They told me I had probably suffered a great deal of stress and anxiety in my job as well as reacting to the bad physical conditions.

There was certainly some improvement in my condition and I was discharged from the hospital, though I had to return from time to time for further treatment and medication. All this time, my sister had been responsible for my expenses and I stayed on in Tientsin afterwards. We were able to visit the museum properly and I found it all most interesting. Unfortunately, the many undisciplined Red Guards who were in Peking at that time had destroyed many of the beautiful ancient things. The Government officials had enclosed the exhibits in barbed wire to protect them from further vandalism, so it was not easy to see them clearly.

I was glad to have the time to visit Peking because as well as being the capital, it was the centre of Chinese civilization.

I went into my sister's room one day while I was staying in her home in Tientsin. She was singing a song about the Great Wall. Xuan had a clear voice and I listened for quite a while.

'What are you singing about?' I asked her. I knew there had always been many old songs abouat the Great Wall.

'Oh, this is not one of the old songs,' she replied. 'This is quite modern. This is about the thousands of stubborn stones that were piled on each other to protect our boundaries from the barbarians. There used to be soldiers and horses that used to patrol inside and outside the walls but today it's all deserted.

'The writer of the song is asking a question,' she went on. 'Was it a sin to build this wall? Was the Emperor wrong? Who can tell if it was right or wrong? In thousands of years it will all be forgotten.'

'I don't think it will. How long has it lasted already? Do you know when it was built?' I asked.

'No, I don't know,' Xuan Linh said. 'I'm not interested in history. But my husband is; he knows all the old legends about the building of the Wall. We'll ask him.'

And later that evening we did ask Binh.

'It was built about 210 BC' he told us. 'It was built as a defence against the barbarians. Many men sacrificed their lives in building and defending it. It winds for about 1500 miles over the mountains and down into the valleys.'

'Hung told us a bit about it,' I replied, 'but it's more interesting when you are living in the place. I didn't really listen before. Is it very high?'

'Oh, yes,' Binh said eagerly. 'In some parts of it, it's as high as twenty feet and the road is quite broad too . . . about thirteen feet. You must go and see it while you are here.'

'What, all fifteen hundred miles of it?' I laughed.

'Let's go and see the Wall on Saturday,' suggested Xuan Linh. 'Do you think you feel well enough, Sang?'

I was feeling much better but I was very thoughtful before I went. I thought about the terribly hard work I had done for the Government, translating for the map-makers in the forests and the mountains; how I had lost my health through it, as had many of the engineers too. Then I thought that perhaps those maps would go on for ever, like the Great Wall, and people would be grateful to us for all our hard work. So though it has cost us a great deal, the results of our work would last for ever. But it needed a poet to write a song about what we had done! I would have to talk to Thu Thuy!

When I actually stood on part of the Wall that weekend, I felt smaller than I had ever felt in my life. It was not the size of the Wall, though that impresed me; it was a sense of the agelessness and continuity of it.

'It's like a huge dragon,' I mused. 'And it goes on and on encircling the mountains . . . I know the answer to that question now. I am sure it was *not* a sin to build the Wall.'

Ever since that time, when I have been tempted to grumble, thinking of my lost health and the spoilt years of my life, I can see that Great Wall still stretching onward, still standing as a symbol of sacrifice and labour.

If I had felt small while standing on the GreatWall, I felt even smaller in the Square of Heavenly Peace in front of the Imperial Palace in Peking. But this was an uncomfortable feeling, not one of awe. The Square in front of the Gate was so immense, so cool, so splendid with its beautiful paving and pictures of ancient Chinese wars and revolutions, but it was ruined by the millions of Red Guards marching about. Even they seemed to be swallowed up in the hugeness.

Everything about the area was the direct opposite of its name. There was no peace at all. The Square had come to stand for the power of the State, the splendour of the Emperor. All was grey . . . a weird greyish-blue probably made even more desolate by the cold, dreary weather. And somehow so empty! Even with all the masses of people, it appeared hollow, void . . .

The soldiers were in their drab military green uniform, while all the Red Guards wore Mao badges and hats; the enormous poster bearing the Chairman's picture dominated everything. As I looked, it seemed to follow me round wherever I stood. These huge pictures of Mao Tse-tung were everywhere at this time.

'This Square has been a place for protests and for political meetings,' Xuan Linh told me, 'as well as for the markets that you can see today.'

There was one very good thing at the time of the Cultural Revolution and that was the cheap food. In

Peking and Tientsin I could buy a large basinful of tomatoes for the equivalent of about seven English pence! It was the first time I had tasted raw tomatoes and I bought so many that I could not eat them all.

My sister and her husband used to go out to work each day, leaving me with about seventeen pence for the day's food. At first I thought, Oh dear! I can't get much to eat with that! But I was wrong. For seven pence I bought three large baskets full of Chinese cabbage. It was so heavy, I could hardly carry it home. Pork, beef and mutton were only twelve pence a pound. When I thought of the difficulty of getting enough food to eat in Vietnam, I felt so sorry for my family there. I began to grow strong again at Xuan Linh's house; I enjoyed the different kinds of food she provided. My sister had grown like the Chinese people in her cooking.

'We know which foods are hot and which are cold,' she said. I knew a little about this from my grandfather's medicine shop; he used to explain it to me. Some foods had a cold effect, even if they were taken hot; for example, tea was cool whether we drank it hot or cold, and all vegetables were either hot or cold. If we had too much hot air in our stomachs, we needed more cool foods to put it right.

'Bananas are neither hot nor cold but I give them to you, Sang, as a laxative,' Xuan Linh told me. (She had given me a great number of bananas.)

'Oh,' I said, laughing, 'I thought you were all very fond of bananas.'

'And when we have the Chinese New Year,' she went on, 'we always eat lots of fried, oily foods and they are too hot. That is why we also eat cool fruits at that time and drink cool drinks.'

'It is very interesting,' I remarked.

'It is very important,' she corrected me, 'and you are a Chinese man too, Sang, even if you are living in Vietnam. You need to know all these things. Our grandfather would not like to think his family had forgotten all the things he knew and practised in his lifetime. We have to carry it on.'

I was glad to be reminded of my grandfather. He had always been an important figure in my life. He had been born in China and knew and loved the old ways and knowledge.

'We cook all our food so that it will do you good as well as fill you up,' Xuan Linh concluded. You don't need medicine as well.'

Unfortunately, I did need medicine as well. Although I felt stronger physically, I kept getting ill. There was something wrong with my heart as well as my kidneys, but they did not give me any treatment for my heart at all. The hospital doctors gave me the secret of the medicine they were giving me, with instructions on how to make it myself at home. Chinese medicines are as difficult as Chinese medical terms to translate into English, but it was a kind of herbal remedy made from roots and leaves and orange peel. It was very cheap to make. I became my own doctor and was able to heal other people too.

Later, I applied to go to South China, as Peking was terribly cold in the winter months. My application was refused. My visitor's visa did not give me the right to stay in China at all, but the authorities in Peking wanted me there to work as an interpreter, so they fought for me to stay. They failed because my family was not from Peking, so in 1968 I returned to Vietnam. I had been in China for two whole years.

3: Changes

Something had happened to me while I had been away from home. I had suffered a great deal physically, but this was not new. I had been ill so often and doctors and hospitals had become part of my life. I think I had gained a vision of real life; it was as if all my emotions and sympathies had been broadened. I had felt, perhaps for the first time, that I was a Chinese man with a great and splendid heritage behind me.

I now recognised the determination of my grandfather in leaving China to start a new life in a new land. I realised the toughness of my parents and admired them for their success, instead of just taking it for granted. Like Hung, I had even gained a sense of respect for our past; great Chinese literature and history meant more to me and even the ancient teachings began to make some sense to me.

I had always been interested in people, but now I cared for them in a different way. I experienced sympathy for our suffering Vietnamese people. I now became increasingly aware of the changes brought about by Communist rule. I believe my parents and brothers had noticed the alterations immediately, but it took me two years away from home and a great deal of physical suffering before I became sufficiently unselfish to see these things for myself.

The first major change I noticed was the wide-spread fear in Nam Dinh. We Vietnamese had become used to being a French colony. We were used to strict rule, and had grown to expect it. But the French, though arrogant and over-bearing, had allowed us to carry on with our own work in our own way. All this was now changed.

The streets had always been happy, busy places, bustling with life. They were almost as important to us as our houses. As soon as we were dressed we used to go out on to the streets, where we might perhaps visit the barber or the dentist, who worked out of doors. Or we would stand and gaze entranced as the fortune tellers carried on their trade. And in the evenings the women and grandmothers would throw the latest baby onto their backs and walk out onto the street, discussing their families and buying snacks at the cafés or restaurants. The Vietnamese were not great drinkers, though they enjoyed beer which they bought at the coffee shops in the country and at the restaurants in the towns.

This had all changed. Most of the street work, which was carried on privately, was forbidden. Everything had to be centralised. Dentists were forced to practise only in the clinics, under Communist eyes and control. Fortune tellers were banned; they threatened our rulers too much. But, though many activities and jobs were forbidden, they still went on underground. This is what accounted for the fear. Everyone was afraid their clandestine practices would leak out. Trust was banished along with the forbidden activities, and the old carefree attitudes were replaced by suspicion. This was not only suspicion of the Communists, our rulers, but of each other. Each of us was weighing up our neighbours to measure the extent of their loyalty.

'I'm afraid of you and you're afraid of me and we're all afraid of each other,' became true of the North Vietnamese.

Many of our old customs and festivals were forbidden too. All plays and operas were banned unless they were influenced by Communist thought, and the sad part of this was that one could grow used to this and not recognise it for what it was.

'This is real indoctrination,' I said to Hung and he agreed.

'Have you seen the children's books used in the Middle School?' he asked me, and he explained that not only the history books but every area of life in Vietnam had become coloured by Communism.

'Officially, there is supposed to be no indoctrination in the Primary Schools,' Hung went on. 'But just look at this book of Bau's!' Bau was Hung's eldest boy.

It was true. Even the simple folk tales carried the imprint of Communism. And the small children would have no standard by which to judge. They would accept what they were taught.

'What about the teachers?' I asked. I had thought a great deal of my teachers in Hanoi Middle School. 'Surely they will remain true to their old beliefs.'

'It's not their fault, Sang,' my brother told me sadly. 'If they don't conform, they lose their jobs. It's as simple as that! And as for the new teachers who are in training now, they have to realise that politics come first. If they fail their politics exams, they lose their jobs. The Communists don't like the professional people anyway. We threaten them . . .' And with that remark I saw a glimpse of the old arrogant Hung. He threw out his chest and said proudly, '*That's* why they forced me to leave University. They feel threatened by me . . . one of the underdogs; they're afraid of me!'

'And there are no small businesses at all now,' put in Thanh. 'When you left for China, there were still a few, weren't there? But now there has been a complete take-over.'

'However hard we work, we shall never be allowed to get rich again,' Hung finished, as he went out to do his boring manual job, with bitterness and frustration. Even his little boy could have done the work Hung was forced to do. I really felt for Hung. Previously I had just been proud of him as my clever brother, but now I could understand his feelings, and enter into them.

All church services were now forbidden. The one Evangelical church in Hanoi, which was very small, had been left open but it might as well have been closed. No one wanted to go, because the Communists had sent a representative from China, and none of the Vietnamese trusted him. The Roman Catholics had been very strong, so the Communists soon put a stop to their activities. All house meetings were forbidden, whether Christian or Buddhist. This did not affect our family but we still sympathised with our Buddhist friends.

My father knew I was interested in writing and he warned me against writing anything that might get me imprisoned.

'There's a very severe penalty for writing anything against the Government,' he said. 'Be careful what you say and what you write. You never know who may become your enemy.'

This made me angry but I understood only too well. 'It was the same in Peking and Tientsin,' I answered him sadly. 'In the restaurants we used to speak almost in whispers. We never knew who was watching and listening. Once some people who had criticised the food were questioned and given a strict warning.'

I had made many close friends in China, and on my return I wrote to them, but I never had one letter back. I knew this was because of the political restrictions. Every letter had to be censored, even between Chinese outside the country. And now it was to be the same in Vietnam.

At this time the war was raging in North Vietnam, with heavy bombing by the Americans. I looked back with amazement to my careless life before the restrictions had begun. I did not seem to be the same young man who had cycled around with Vinh. I had said then that the Government had nothing to do with our private everyday lives! Now it seemed that every part of our lives had disintegrated. There was no peace in our country; there could be no peace in our hearts or homes.

With all this happening around me, I had no time to think much of my health. Everyone at home thought I was better, though I knew that the root of the trouble was not really solved. I did not want to worry my mother unnecessarily. She looked even sadder and was quieter than before I had gone away. Thu Thuy had been right as usual. I realised now that my little sister had certainly grown up before me. But now I understood, and how I wished I did not! It was a knowledge that could give no pleasure.

In December 1968 a new problem arose. I had woken one night and picked up a torch. It dropped to the ground. Every time I picked it up, I dropped it again. I felt very strange. There was a heavy feeling all down one side of my body, and I found I could not hold on to anything.

About two o'clock in the morning, I woke my father and told him. 'I can't hold on to anything,' I said.

'Well, don't try to hold on to anything!' he said. He didn't understand and I could not explain. 'Just go to sleep! You'll be all right in the morning.'

But in the morning I couldn't get up. I was unable to move at all. I was completely paralysed.

Then my father *was* worried. 'The boy's had a stroke,' he said. I could see he thought I was dying. He called an ambulance and they rushed me to the hospital. I was put into an emergency ward and given an injection. This brought me round, but I still couldn't move at all. I could not feed myself. My family thought that it was the end of me. But I was determined that I was not going to die. I didn't feel there was anything wrong with me. Although I was paralysed, I felt quite well in myself. I could think clearly.

'I'm not going to die yet,' I told them. However, I was in that hospital for a month. Slowly I became able to move one hand, and I kept practising. I grabbed the bed and shuffled around. I determined to go on trying to walk. I was far too young to be paralysed.

'If I can't walk,' I said to the nurses, 'I might as well

die; in fact it would be better to die.'

So I practised every day. Soon I could walk with a stick. I felt there was no need for me to stay in the hospital. I could practise walking at home while my father and mother were working. They had to work very hard at this time, for otherwise our food supplies would be cut off by the Government officials. Life in Vietnam was becoming more and more difficult. But I was still alive, in spite of the prophecies of the doctors!

There followed a period of my life that I can't remember very well. All the days and months seem to run into each other. From 1968, when I returned home to Nam Dinh till 1978, when we made our decision to leave Vietnam, my chief memories are of constant illness, feeling very weak and being a nuisance to my family. Looking back now, I don't think I want to remember much of it. At that time, medicine and doctors and hospitals were far more important to me than politics and the Government.

My main ambition was to get well. 'I must get really well,' I said to my mother over and over. She must have grown tired of hearing me say the same thing so often.

One day I overheard my father talking about my illness. 'Sang won't ever get better,' he said. 'We might as well get used to the idea. He will always be paralysed. If he were going to improve, he would have regained the use of his hand and arm by now.'

He was not unkind about it. He was just stating a fact. It was the same as if I had said that my brother Thanh would always be curious about electrical and mechanical things, or that my sister Thu Thuy would always be scribbling poetry, even in the midst of difficulties.

My mother was sad about me, I knew. I had always been the strongest of the family. My future had seemed so promising.'Keep on trying,' she would beg me. 'I believe that you can get a little better. Keep practising walking every day!'

There was no need for her to encourage me. I spent the whole of every day trying to exercise my hand and practising walking. But progress was very slow. Because of my illness I was left out of some of the family conferences that were going on at that time. But when I found out what they were planning, I was with them all the way.

The family had been discussing the possibility of leaving Vietnam ever since 1954, when the Communists took over.

My father really suffered from losing his status as a prosperous business man. The shop was completely different under Government control. No one stood around chatting as they bought.

My mother suffered because it was hard to get enough to eat, and because she saw her grandchildren becoming little Communist puppets without even realising it. They said what they were told to say and did what was expected of them. Obedience to the Government was the most important thing in their small lives.

Hung suffered from wild frustration and anger. He loathed the manual work he was forced to do. He hadn't even liked helping when the store was ours, or helping in Grandfather's medicine shop. He was a student at heart and loved learning. The Government had overturned all his ambitions.

'There is no freedom at all,' he said passionately. 'No freedom of speech, or of writing, of working . . . in fact, no freedom to live or be ourselves.'

'I think we'll have to leave Vietnam,' my father said and though there was regret in his voice, there was firm resolution too. 'Others are leaving by boat. And the time is *now*, while the Government still wants us to go. They may clamp down on that soon!'

The fear had intensified. The whole of our lives seemed to be governed by fear and suspicion. The anger that most of us felt towards the Communists was merely one of the consequences of fear.

When I managed to forget my paralysis and take a critical look round our home, our shop, our whole neighbourhood, it struck me how utterly different it had become! The happy, carefree street life was a thing of the past; family visits to friends were over; the sharing of joys and sorrows was very constrained; our standard of living was lower; there were bans on our festivities and all business life was centralised. The closure of churches and the forbidding of services and house meetings did not affect us personally as we were not a religious family, but it hurt us to see our friends deprived of their religious freedom. To them it did matter.

Things were difficult for all the Vietnamese people, but at that time they were particularly bad for families like ours, who were of Chinese origin. There were conflicts between the Vietnamese and Chinese Government, and Chinese people became very unpopular with the Government, particularly perhaps, because many of them had been successful business people before 1954. Now we were regarded as possible security risks, and were also under suspicion of being American sympathisers.

At that time the Government was positively encouraging families like ours to leave, but always at the back of our minds there was a growing fear that if we inadvertently offended the Government, we might possibly be sent to the New Economic Zones, or imprisoned. The prospect was bleak.

4: Voyage to Freedom

It was early in 1978 that we made our great decision to leave Vietnam. The troubles between the Chinese and the Government grew worse and we felt that there was no future for any of us. It wasn't that they actually chased us out, but they said, 'If you want to leave, we'll allow you to.'

'We will all go,' said my father sternly, 'I will not leave one of you behind. If we cannot raise enough money for us all, we will stay here.'

All the same, there were many difficulties about going as well as staying. We would need a great deal of gold to enable us to sail to Hong Kong. That is where we planned to go, though it would be only a temporary stop. We wanted to go to America, where one of my brothers was already happily settled. At first we thought it would be simple to sell our two houses and use the gold to buy a strong boat to take us. We knew we should have to include another family with some knowledge of seamanship to captain us over the South China Sea. The voyage would take about five days if the weather was good.

But there were so many hindrances and disappointments.

One day my father came in with a tragic expression on his face. 'What is it?' we all asked. 'What has happened?'

He flung himself down on his bed. 'It's no good. They won't let us sell our houses. All these years we've worked for them and now – if we go – we will have to leave our houses for them.'

'But they are ours,' wailed my mother. 'We bought them ourselves from all our hard work.'

'*And*they said we could go,' protested Hung. 'They know we can't go without a boat.'

My father's face was full of anger. 'Oh yes, they'll let us go,' he shouted. 'We can all go. We can leave our own land as long as we leave all our possessions behind for *them*. We have to go as refugees, not as free agents at all.'

'Well, I want to go,' said Hung stoutly. 'I want to go all the more. I want to go where we can be free: free to work as we wish, free to live as we wish, free to study as we wish.'

Hung's frustration had been bottled up in him for so long. Thu Thuy was crying quietly. She didn't make a sound. The tears just poured down her face.

'Well, I want to go too,' she whispered. 'But how do we know if we shall be free in America? Everything we have is here . . . and Vietnam is a beautiful country. I love the birds and flowers and our splendid parks. And all our friends are here.'

'We will make new friends,' I comforted her. I was very fond of Thu Thuy. She had been especially kind to me since I had been ill. 'You will always make friends wherever you go. And we shall all be together.

Remember, we are not going to split up our family.'

'Our family has begun to be split up already,' she replied, and it was true. My sister Ha Anh and her family were living in Hong Kong and my second brother was in America. Xuan Linh was in China.

'And Grandfather and Grandmother are both dead,' Thu Thuy went on. She always did a lot of talking but usually she was happy and hopeful. Now her pretty face looked quite pathetic and her small children clung to her and cried too.

'Now stop it, all of you!' My father spoke irritably. He was too worried to care about details. The responsibility was all on him and he had to act fast.

'Listen,' he said. 'The officials said we could sell our

possessions apart from our houses: our cups and saucers and pots as well as our radios and bicycles. We can make a little money that way.'

'Our bikes,' grumbled Thanh. 'I wanted to take mine with me.'

'Foolish boy!' My father never had any sympathy with Thanh. He considered him a spoilt, selfish boy, who had never grown up. 'Did you think we could go to another country carting all our possessions with us? If we go at all, we go with a boat and just enough food, drink and clothes for the voyage. We must start to get together as much gold as we can, that is, if we are all agreed that we want to go.'

He looked round at us all. It was quite a solemn moment in the history of our family. My mother agreed. Hung agreed. Thu Thuy agreed. I agreed. Thanh went on muttering.

'Well, I agree too,' he said at last. 'The life here is no good. But no one shall take my radio from me. We shall need that on the boat.'

My father said no more to Thanh. Perhaps he too thought we might need the radio for the weather forecast.

Thu Thuy seemed to find her consolation in her poems. She read some of them to me, as I was still an invalid.

'I read a poem by Lu Xun and I know just how he felt,' she said. 'Listen, Sang!' and she read me a verse she had copied out while she was at Middle School:

My heart had no way to dodge the arrows loosed by
love of country;
Storms weigh down like boulders and darken the
gardens of my homeland;
I pass my message to the chill stars, for my people
don't heed my sorrow.
I pledge to make my own blood my offering to my
native land.

'Do you really feel as strongly as that?' I asked her. 'You would not be a martyr?'

'No, I suppose not,' she admitted, 'but I do love my Vietnam. It does become like an arrow to my heart, the love I have for it.' Then she went on, 'Here, listen! This is my own poem:

And when I dream of a new land
and a home away from home,
I dream always of Vietnam and the fields of golden rice;
with the sky so blue
and the grass green
and the birds like rainbows,
and lotus pink and white and the bamboo tree . . .
all arrows in my heart.

I felt sorry for Thu Thuy but I did not share her emotions. Once we had made the decision to leave, I thought forward, not backward. Forward to the new country . . . our new homeland.

'There will be blue sky and green fields there too,' I assured Thu Thuy, 'and growing things and birds and flowers.'

'Yes . . . all arrows in my heart,' she replied, so I left her to her arrows. I think in one way she was enjoying their sting. Perhaps poets are like that !

After all, Vietnam was her country. She didn't remember living in China at all. None of us did. Our family had left China in Grandfather's early days. He had found it impossible then to make a living and his family was very poor. It was mainly through Grandfather's efforts that we had become rich and prosperous and now it looked as if all his hard work and that of my parents had been for nothing. Once again we were leaving our homeland; once again it looked as if we should go into the unknown with nothing of our own. And we were not returning to China, the home of our ancestors; there was still no place for us there. Perhaps there was no place anywhere for us to make a new home!

One of my little nieces – she was about seven years old – had a rather quaint way of speaking. She said, 'Oh yes, we do have a home. It's just that we have nowhere to put it!'

The months following our decision were busy. We were selling our things and accumulating gold. Other families were doing the same. We made plans with Binh, a fisherman friend of Hung's. He was used to captaining his own small fishing-boat, and he agreed to come with us with his family of ten. We also invited Cuong, another friend, who had a little knowledge of navigation. The boat was bought, but it was a very small one. It was only thirty foot long and there would be nearly forty people on board. About seventeen of these would be children who, fortunately, would take less space.

Five days in that small space would be terribly uncomfortable and if we had any bad weather . . . well, it would be worse than just uncomfortable! Strangely enough, now that we had the boat and the voyage was almost upon us, we all felt hopeful. The sea had always been good to us; we were happy afloat; we were going in search of freedom and we would all be together. The children were hardly old enough to understand, but they caught our hopefulness and grew excited.

By the time we were all aboard our boat, we were very tired, but at least we were on our way to Hong Kong. It was terribly cramped but we each had a small space and there we had to stay. There was little room to move about and whenever the boat rolled, we fell on top of each other. At first the children thought this was great fun, but after little Nghe had been trodden on by Thanh's large foot, there were tears as well as laughter. And then there was no more laughter for a long time!

For the first two days at sea, Thanh was fiddling with his radio. He had got his way over this, and the rather large radio was clutched to his side, taking up valuable space. Thanh was extremely clever with all electrical things, but there was a fault with this radio and he grew crosser every minute. He seemed to become obsessed with making it work.

'It is important that we get contact,' he kept saying.

'Oh, be quiet!' said my father. 'Leave it! It is not so important as surviving and reaching Hong Kong.'

'I don't think we shall reach Hong Kong without it,' muttered Thanh.

We had left Nam Dinh on a Thursday and on Saturday afternoon, there was a shout from Thanh. 'I've got it. Listen!' Thanh's voice was very excited. His words rang out across the water. Suddenly we heard the voice of the weather reporter. That rang out too, though it was still crackly.

'Typhoon Maria expected; 250 miles south-east of Macau. Force 9-10 . . . increasing.'

We all went very quiet . . . even the small children were silent, looking at us, though they did not understand.

'There! What did I tell you?' Thanh said, but I don't think he had. My niece Nghe, who was six years old, said, 'I wish you had not put that radio right. Then we should still be OK.'

We were used to hearing of typhoons on the South China Sea, but we had never been in a predicament like this. Our boat was far too small and unprepared to meet the typhoon; we had not sufficient navigational expertise to avoid it.

The captain looked grave. My father and brothers were anxious. Even a slight typhoon could be a disaster. But it was better to know that it was coming. The men set about preparing for the storm. The women battened down the water tanks; we dare not lose our drinking supply. I could do nothing to help at all. Normally I would be one of the hardest workers, but I just had to lie there on board like a dead man; I could not move at all. Even if I could have managed to stagger a few steps, the motion of the boat would have soon sent me overboard. It was worse, not being able to do anything, because I had to listen to the children crying. They were all frightened so they kept asking questions that no one could answer. Because I was just lying there, they asked me. I tried to give them some answer.

'Yes, I can see a light ahead. Yes, perhaps it is Hong Kong. Cheer up! We'll soon have plenty to eat and drink.'

But it never was Hong Kong. Sometimes it was a fishing boat a long way off and once we saw a lighthouse. The children gave up asking me questions. They could not trust my answers.

There was still some blue in the sky; the clouds gathered only slowly, but it was not long before we could feel the swell. Our boat began to pitch and toss; the children screamed; they were sick and terrified and they were hurled about from one side to the other. The wind grew stronger and the rain began to lash down from all directions at once. We were drenched to the skin in two minutes.

Of course we had already taken the sails down, and when the north wind hit us, we were blown right off course. The sails were ripped to shreds in seconds and we had to sit on them to keep them in the boat at all.

Then came the time when no one asked questions. No one cried any more. The noise of the wind and sea were too deafening. The hurricane howled in fury. The sky was pitch black, though it was daytime. The sea was black. Our hearts felt black with terror. We sat huddled together, hanging on to the children, tossing about like a cork. We were completely at the mercy of the wild weather.

One second we were right at the bottom of the ocean, or so it seemed; the next we were flung up high and there was just angry sky, with walls of tempestuous water shutting us in. I felt smothered. I felt the breath going out of me. This was sheer horror . . . a continuous nightmare, from which we could not escape . . . there was no awakening. We were too petrified even to think.

When there was a slight lull in the ferocity of the hurricane, we were able to make ourselves heard. My father yelled to me, 'We'll all die together. We shan't get there.' I shouted back to him, 'Yes we will. We shan't drown.'

I don't know why I had so much hope. I was soaking wet, cold and terrified, but I had been very close to death before, and though this typhoon was certainly the worst thing that had ever happened to me, perhaps I was somehow prepared for it. If I had known a god at that time or if my parents had been strong Buddhists, I expect we should have prayed to God or Buddha, but we were all atheists. There was no help for us. The children had given up crying; they were too petrified to move or make a sound at all. But they went on shaking. I could see their teeth chattering.

I remember thinking, There must be something more for me than death by drowning or hunger. Otherwise, why have I been kept alive all this time when the doctors gave me up for dead more than twenty years ago? And this typhoon is terrible, but it could have been worse. We have not capsized . . . yet!

It was true. Typhoon Maria was not one of the fiercest, or perhaps we had somehow managed to avoid the cruellest area. I did not voice my thoughts aloud, even if my family could have heard me above the roar of the storm. They would not have thought it a helpful remark.

About three o'clock one afternoon (I quite forget which day it was), the wind began to grow less violent; the rain became less severe; even the sea was less terrifying, though we were still being tossed about. Was this simply a temporary lull or could it be the beginning of the end of the typhoon? At least we were still alive; still aboard, though we had all taken a serious battering. We were all soaked to the skin; our clothes were sodden all through, but worst of all the food was soaked too. Our boat was knee-deep in icy water. As soon as it was possible for us to move about safely, my father shouted, 'Wake up and get baling!'

There was plenty of work to be done, and it was good to have something to do again. They all worked very hard . . . even the children tried to help ladle out water. I did nothing, but inside I felt happy. We had not capsized. We were alive. I knew now that we should reach Hong Kong. And when, later, the sea itself began to calm a little, even my father's voice had a hopeful ring in it. 'Put up the sail,' he ordered, 'and let's go!' Although he was not the captain, he had bought the boat, so he was in charge.

Binh and Hung mended the torn sails as well as they could, and soon the boat was being controlled by Binh, not by the typhoon.

After the typhoon was over and the sea was moderately calm, we were so relieved that we felt we could bear any discomfort or hardship. We said to each other, 'If we have come out of that alive, we shall be all right now.'

And that is how we felt for a few days, but then the food grew shorter, even the water was almost gone, and the children were very sick. They cried constantly and their crying was really piteous; it was as if they knew there was no hope for them. Their mothers could not help. I think they felt like crying themselves. I know Thu Thuy did. I thought a great deal about my own son, though it was so long since I had seen him. I should have been glad he was not on this cruel sea, but instead it was as if all the other small boys belonged to me and I felt for them all, not having my own son to feel for. I suffered for them.

There was more to come. As the days passed, it was

as though they all ran into each other. Every day was the same. Every day we were wet and cold; we were hungry and thirsty; we were anxious about the future. We worried about the sick ones and the boat grew more and more dirty. The smell was quite dreadful and there was nothing we could do about it. We were too crowded together to get it cleaned up. The women tried but the children were constantly sick and the buckets used for sanitation kept being spilled. If the boat lurched, the contents were spilled on to the people. Some of them were past using the buckets anyway. The women were feeling too ill to care; none of us felt well.

My mother looked dreadful. I think she had suffered for her whole family, especially as there was nothing she could do for them. At the back of my head, I heard her saying, over and over, like the chorus in a song. 'Don't cry! Don't cry! Don't cry!' I could hear it in my mind even when she was not saying it.

One day, after what seemed like weeks or months, we sighted a vessel in the distance. As it came nearer, we saw that it was a big ship.

'Perhaps there is hope for us,' said my father. 'Let's hail it and ask for help!'

'It may be an enemy,' replied Binh who was more cautious. 'We are better on our own.'

The ship came nearer; there was no need for us to hail it. They shouted to us in Cantonese. They had good news for us. 'You are nearly at Hong Kong,' they assured us. 'You'll be all right now. We will give you a tow into the harbour.'

They gave us some biscuits and water, so the children were happy again. They thought all their troubles were over, but it was not to be as easy as that!

There we were, right out in the middle of the ocean; we could see no land at all. We had to trust the sailors and they were not willing to tow us into the harbour for nothing.

'You must give us gold,' they insisted, though their

manner was still kind. We trusted them because there was nothing else we could do. 'We can't do it for nothing. There may be others wanting a tow. It takes times and money.'

We thought, Well, what value is our money to us if we can't get into the harbour?

We were right at the end of our resources. We had had our fill of discomforts; if they left us, there might be another typhoon, worse than the last; we could easily die of hunger or thirst. I felt too ill to care, anyway, and the responsibility of the two families was weighing down my father. So we handed over all our gold . . . all our careful savings. Once they knew we had gold at all, there was no holding any of it back. We had no time to think of the state of utter destitution we should be in when we arrived in Hong Kong. All we cared about was that we should get there. *They* would not let us starve. We had friends there already, as well as my sister Ha Anh and her family.

So we set off with the ship towing us along. Once they had their hands on our gold, they didn't seem to care about us any more. They dragged us along at the pace of their ship, and our boat was so small that it nearly sank. It was terrifying.

'Stop! Stop!' we yelled to them, but either they could not hear or preferred not to, for they still went on dragging us with them. Our boat filled up again with water. It was almost as dangerous as the typhoon, but Hung kept on saying, 'It doesn't matter now. At least we shan't be drowned. At least we're nearing Hong Kong all the time. At least we can dry out in Hong Kong.'

But he only spoke to reassure himself. I could see he was afraid and he was a tough man. My mother was terrified; she made little wailing noises. The boat was tossing about at the end of the rope. This went on for one whole hour and still we could see nothing . . . no lights . . . no land.

At the end of an hour, the men stopped their ship. They shouted to us, 'You're nearly at Hong Kong now. You'll be all right.' Our hearts sank. We had heard those words before. The sailors threw us some canvas in case of more storms. They cut the rope and they left us. We were alone again, alone on the dark sea and for all we knew, as far away from land as ever, much wetter and much poorer. It was strange, but we didn't think of the sailors' deceit or wickedness at that time. All we thought about was how we should survive.

'Well,' said Thanh, 'at least we have some water now. I didn't like the idea of dying of thirst.'

'And they did leave us plenty of biscuits,' said my mother, doling some out to the children.

'The canvas may come in useful,' Father remarked, 'but I hope we shan't have to use it.'

It was as if all of us were determined to make the best of it. Even saying these things made us feel better. After all, it was quite true; they had left us some necessities. Some families we had heard about had far worse things happen to them. At least our men had not been brutal.

'I think we shall get to Hong Kong,' I said, and I clung on to that hope all that night. I had to cling on to something. I could not hold on to anything with my hands; they were quite useless, so I clung on with my mind. *That* was still very clear. It was as clear as the water, which grew greener as we sailed nearer to land. Thu Thuy said, 'Look, the sea is the same colour as my grandmother's jade bracelet.' (This was one thing that had not been sold to get gold.) 'It is quite different here from the navy-blue water, just before the typhoon. It is transparent.'

I was the only one who listened to Thu Thuy. She talked on and on. The words were like liquid pouring out of a bottle. She had always been like this in Vietnam. I think she was a little like me. I liked words too and my little niece, Nghe, Thu Thuy's eldest daughter, was going to be the same one day. But I couldn't help thinking that Thu Thuy was strange to talk so poetically at such a time. The others were far too busy to notice Thu Thuy's talk. All they cared about was reaching Hong Kong as soon as possible.

I can't remember which day we eventually saw real harbour lights in the distance. At first we refused to believe the evidence of our eyes; we had had too many disappointments. But when we saw the outline of buildings on the skylines, we were thrilled.

It was almost evening. We felt light-hearted for the first time for a whole month. '*Surely* it must be the real thing this time,' said my mother. She looked terribly thin and ill; she had hardly eaten anything and I think she had been more frightened than any of us. But now her eyes had hope in them.

We all began to shout. We shouted till we were hoarse. The sea was calm now. One of my little nephews, Hung's eldest boy, who had been very seasick and had suffered from bad nightmares, just lay on the boards and sang out, 'Hong Kong . . . Hong Kong . . . Hong Kong!' like a chorus. It reminded me of the chanting of my mother, 'Don't cry! Don't cry'! earlier, but this chorus had hope in it.

Thu Thuy's little girl, Nghe, was still too ill to care. Her face looked small and pinched and she was filthy. Even her hair was all matted. She had always been my favourite niece, full of fun and such a chatterbox in Vietnam. I had wanted to have a daughter like Nghe, but today I could hardly recognise her. While all the shouting and excitement was going on, Nghe crept closer to me. Her floor space had been near mine but I could not reach out to her. She put her cold,wet little hand into my limp one. And so we waited, saying nothing. There was plenty being said by all the rest.

It wasn't long before we noticed a Police boat following us. 'Where have you come from?' they shouted to us. 'From Vietnam,' we shouted back.

A hush fell over our boat. The men were in uniform,

and the women and children were afraid. They spoke Cantonese all right, but there was a difference in the *way* they spoke it. Their accent was more aggressive. They had a job to do and there was no time to be polite. They came aboard our dirty little boat, bringing a grappling iron with them. We knew there was no need to fear this time. They would tow us with care and in a professional manner.

And so, at last, after one long month on the South China Sea, we were sailing right up into the harbour and it was a beautiful evening. We saw the famous Connaught Building, of which we had seen pictures. It was beautiful. *Everything* was beautiful. The blocks of skyscrapers were beautiful. Night was coming on, and the whole scene was illuminated. The lights were like millions of diamonds but all different colours, sparkling and brilliant. Then we saw movement, and way up the mountains, the road lights were bright and traffic was moving. I think now that these lights may have come from the Tai-ping mountains, but to us then, as we were still being escorted by the Police boat, they were all just part of Hong Kong, our haven.

Binh, Cuong and my father and brothers were bustling about, preparing to disembark; my mother was collecting the children's wet things; Hung was trying to tell anyone who would listen everything he knew about the mountains – 'they mean great peace to the city,' he said – and Thu Thuy was crying softly.

'It is all too beautiful,' she said. 'This is the most beautiful city in the world and so colourful. But I feel as if I am a traitor to my homeland. To be happy away from home is to be a traitor. Only . . . the torrent . . . the terror . . . the typhoon are all behind us, and the wild, wild waves.'

I had been expecting her to burst into poetry again but she said there would be time enough for that later on when the family had found a new home . . . somewhere. She quoted instead from another poem that she was always saying by heart . . . a poem by the great Chinese poet Lang Youwei. This was about the Jewish people in Jerusalem at the Wailing Wall, that was said to have been built by Solomon. They had been a suffering people too, like the Chinese and the Vietnamese and many more; they too had faced disasters for 2,000 years as a nation . . . they too had a great and deep feeling of love for their homeland.

'I like these two lines, don't you Sang?' Thu Thuy asked me.

One can never abandon one's native country or rest
for ever undisturbed;
I remain always a Chinese man, looking in the
direction of my former home;

'Yes, I like that,' I agreed and then she did burst out with a poem of her own. It is a pity it has to be translated into English.

It is true . . . I will never abandon my native home
I will always be Chinese within me;
I will always look back to Vietnam,
my home, the home of my ancestors,
the home of my childhood and youth
where I was wife and mother . . .

But Hong-Kong beckons me and America maybe
and I look on too to the new home,
the home that is a question mark, an unknown
blank
for me to fill . . .

I looked at Thu Thuy. Her eyes were alight; hope was shining inside her and brightening her face. She had been a very good sister to me. I loved her, and she gave me hope. My past held so much that was bad and painful and my present was uncertain and uncomfortable. There was only the future for me. The unknown future . . . a blank for me to fill. I was so thankful our family was to stay together. Without them I would feel very lost.

I felt almost poetical myself. I remembered one line of an ancient Chinese poem. I think it was written by Wen Yiduo in a collection of poems called *Dead Water*. The only line I could recall was:

Out of dead water a song will rise.

Trying to show Thu Thuy that I understood her feelings, I said it to her. 'Oh, I remember that line too,' she said excitedly. 'We had to write it as an exercise in writing Chinese characters. I found the book and learnt some more. It is a beautiful poem.'

So this ditch of hopeless dead water
May well boast a certain splendour . . .

That is what the poet is saying,' she went on joyfully. 'Beauty is always alive . . . it can't be killed. Even in the midst of that terrible tyhphoon I noticed the sea-colour . . . that deep purply navy-blue, only a song of terror came from that water . . . but here, sailing smoothly up the harbour, with this clear green water, our song is one of relief and gratitude and joy to come.'

I thought it very strange that I should be listening and remembering ancient poetry at such a time; there was so much going on, such bustle and excitement . . . so much action. But I was forced to be inactive and Thu Thuy was nursing little Nghe and it seemed fitting.

I remember thinking, I wish we could stay here for ever. Hong Kong *is* beautiful. But I knew that Hong Kong was one of the busiest and most highly populated cities in the world too, full of bright lights and noise and traffic and peoples of all kinds. As we landed, they were swarming everywhere.

The police ushered us into a huge room where there were several hundred people, and every one of them was a refugee. We did not tell our story because every one of them had a story to tell. We were just glad to be there, safe and dry.

They gave us a good meal. We were able to get clean at last and have a proper sleep. It was such a treat to be able to stretch out our legs, without knocking someone else on the head. My mother found she could not stretch hers out; they had grown stiff in the sitting position. She cried out with pain when she tried to move them.

This was a detention centre, but it was our haven. We didn't want to think of the future . . . yet!

5: Hong Kong

It was not long before we *had* to think of the future. Refugees were pouring into the camp every day, some of them in very poor shape. Some of the women were pregnant and many had to stay in hospital. The overcrowding was terrible but we were safe, for the present.

At first, while all the registration was going on, we were restricted to the detention centre. It did not worry me because I still could not move, but the rest of my family did a lot of complaining.

'We must apply to go to America,' they said. 'We are like a lot of flies here.'

'We need clothes,' worried my mother.

'I wish we had more to eat,' complained the boys.

But my mother would not let them grumble about the food. We were not starving, though we felt hungry quite often, but then we were used to that. Even in Vietnam we had not always had enough to eat. 'You boys, be thankful!' Mother ordered.

I kept thinking about my older sister Ha Anh, who was in Hong Kong already with her family. I was sure she would help us. We longed to see her, but it was awkward to ask for favours, because everyone needed something and we were among the 'OK' ones. That's what they called us, although I did not feel very OK! Someone in our family (I forget who it was) managed to write a note, and then screwed it up small and threw it to someone who was passing the camp. Ha Anh's address was on it. Then we waited. Would Ha Anh ever get the note? Would she be allowed into the camp? After all, we were not allowed out of it . . . yet!

'I must see Ha Anh, I must,' said my mother. 'We may go off to America soon and then we'll never see her and the children again.'

'She will come,' I said and I didn't say it just to comfort her. I was quite sure she would find a way in somehow. I always felt hopeful, even though I was still so ill. Now that we had reached Hong Kong safely after that dreadful month on the sea, I was certain that everything would be all right.

Thu Thuy was very depressed. She had been so excited when we arrived, but now she had become very quiet. She was worried about little Nghe who was still ill and eating almost nothing. The doctor had seen her, and given her some medicine. 'You must give her time to get over the voyage,' he said.

After a few days of anxious waiting, Ha Anh did arrive. Oh, it was good to see her, especially as it was the first time we had seen anyone from outside the camp. She looked fit and well, but seeing me so ill and little Nghe so pale and small, she burst into tears.

'Oh Sang,' she cried, 'you were always my strong brother. What has happened? You have shrunk.'

Everyone talked at once and there was a lot of laughing and crying. Ha Anh promised to bring in all sorts of things; food and clothes and shoes for the children, but the authorities restricted the amount of food brought in. I suppose they thought it would cause jealousy.

However, Ha Anh's visit did cheer Thu Thuy. She began to chat again and be more like the Thu Thuy we all knew. My mother too felt more resigned to leaving now that she had seen her daughter and found her well and happy.

We were now moved into one of the refugee camps. We were glad to see the back of the detention centre, though we had been pleased enough to be there at first.

It had been our refuge, but we were eager for the next move. It made us feel that *something* was being planned for us.

Our camp was called Jubilee and it was next door to the Sham Sui Po camp, in fact we could talk to each other over the fences. Our back doors looked out on to the water-front and further round, you could just see a glimpse of the ferry to Kowloon.

Jubilee was a very, very old building. People said it was haunted! There were several hundred bunk beds in it and it was a grey and gloomy building, in spite of the many windows. But at least our family could be together and we had a small space which was our own. We did not grumble. We knew it was only for a short time.

After a while, everyone was allowed outside the camp and it was up to them to find work. There were plenty of factories wanting workers: electronics, watch and radio factories. Thanh was soon very busy working with digital watches. I could not go outside the camp because of my physical handicap. Apart from the paralysis, my heart was bad and I was tired all the time.

When my family returned from their work they used to tell me about Hong Kong. They talked about the markets under the huge apartment buildings; all kinds of food were sold there and after about five o'clock, there were snacks for people to buy and eat. Hong Kong was a noisy place; even inside the refugee camp with the doors closed, I could hear the constant roar of traffic, clanking of cranes and noises from the building sites. It was never really quiet.

'You are better in here,' my mother said to comfort me. 'Out there it is all tension . . . people racing to catch buses . . . over-crowded buses too . . . long, long queues . . . queues for the shops and for the cinemas.'

My father and brothers painted a different picture. 'It is exciting,' Thanh told me, as he returned from his first week at the digital watch factory. I think he was the happiest of all my family at that time. He loved the work and he had never worried much about the future. He left all the worrying to my father.

'I like the speed of this place,' Thanh told me, 'and the record shops are fabulous. The cinemas are good too.'

His wife Lam said to him, 'Don't spend all the money you earn. Remember, we have to make a home in the new country. Remember your children!' Thanh shrugged his shoulders and laughed. He felt rich and healthy and happy.

'Don't worry!' he said. 'We'll be all right. I can always make lots of money.'

Lam sighed. Life in Jubilee was not much fun for her. She had always been very particular about cleanliness, and the crowded conditions in the camp made washing and cooking difficult.

One day the police escorted me to the hospital, where I was given a thorough overhaul. They discovered the state of my heart and said I would have to have an operation.

My first emotion was fear. I was really afraid of an operation. I had been very ill for a long time, and had had a lot of treatment both in Vietnam and in Peking Hospital. I was quite paralysed in my right arm and leg, but an operation was something new to me. I felt a long way from home. My family obviously thought that I was finished.

Eventually I said, 'OK, I have got to die some time. I will have the operation.'

That is what I said out loud, but inside myself I thought that perhaps I might get well after all. I still had some hope in me. After all, the Vietnamese doctors had given me up long ago and here I was, still alive!

While all this was happening, I had applied to go to America with my family but after waiting for several months, we still had no news. It seemed that America did not want us, or maybe they had too many refugees already.

Thanh wanted to go to Canada and my father, seeing

how ill I was and having to wait for the operation, applied to go there instead. It took some time but eventually all my family were accepted by the Canadian authorities – all except me. The Canadians did not want an invalid on their hands.

My family set off towards their new life where they hoped to be able to gain some kind of livelihood. I saw them all go . . . my father and mother, my brothers and their wives and children, my sister Thu Thuy, my nieces and nephews. My throat felt sore with sadness and my heart was heavy as lead. Would I ever see my mother again? Who would take care of me? Would the operation be successful? What was going to happen to me? *They* were all together. I was alone.

I felt very desolate . . . very lonely. I was now just one person alone with no family. There was no one to rely on any more. I felt my hope ebbing away. Was my life ebbing away too? I did not mind if it was at this time. I was not angry with my family: my parents had to find a home for their children and grandchildren; it was their responsibility. I know my mother wanted to stay, but there was no place for her in Hong Kong. It was hard for her too. I was her son and I was very ill.

Then one day some American missionaries arrived at the refugee camp. There were at least sixty of them and when they came, there was nothing they would not do. They cleaned the drains. They swept the floors. I thought, This is very strange. They are all dressed so nicely, but they are willing to do this kind of work.

The toilets were just metal boxes that kept overflowing, and no one wanted to empty them. They were so dreadful that I did not dare to go in at all, but the American ladies cleaned and emptied them. I really admired them. I wished I could speak to them and thank them, but I knew no English. I could not understand why they should do such dirty work, and they seemed happy doing it

In fact they were nurses, not cleaners! The interpreters told us that they did the work because they were Christians. The only Christians I had met in North Vietnam were Roman Catholics. They were very strong there, until the Communists closed their churches. There was one 'Tinlanh' church in Hanoi, but it had been closed by the Communists in 1955. The interpreters told us that this church's teaching was more like that of the American missionaries. Apparently it was a Gospel church, but I had never noticed it and knew nothing about it at all.

One day an American lady called Noelle came to see me. She had seen me lying ill in my bunk all day, and she wanted to talk to me. I could not understand what she was saying, though we had an interpreter. I was willing to listen because I thought the missionaries were good people and very kind to the refugees, but I had no idea what it meant to believe in Jesus. I did not know who he was.

Noelle asked me many questions. She wanted to know if I was all right; was I warm enough; did I have enough clothes; did I need any medicine. Then she asked me if I wanted to take part in her Bible Study. I said, 'What is Bible Study?'

I didn't understand what they were saying to me, but I went along to Bible Study. It was somewhere to go. Out of all those hundreds of refugees, only about ten went. They were not believers; they just went to hear. I went to hear and I believed. I believed Jesus because I didn't have anyone else. God saw that I had exhausted my own resources and so He came to save me. That is what I understand now. God saves sinners and those who are sick, and I was very sick.

I will never forget my first real Christian lesson. It was the Parable of the Sower. Noelle was talking about this and suddenly it began to make sense. She wrote it up on a board and illustrated it with drawings too. She told us about the different kinds of hearts there were and how they were like the ground that the seed was sown in. She asked us which ground our hearts were like. I said, 'My heart is like number two, the rocky ground where the seed could not put down much root.'

I felt then as if God was planting a seed in my heart and I thought, Well, my heart may not be strong, but it is ready to receive a message. So I listened with all my heart. I attended every day, whenever I could. I was always in the camp because I still could not go out at all.

Sometimes the interpretations were not clear and I could not understand, but I still went. It was not Noelle's fault that I could not understand and what she had to say was always worth hearing.

Some days Noelle talked to me about my future. She advised me to go to England, as neither Canada nor America would have me. I thought, Why should England have me? How could I go there? Who would look after me there? Who would feed me? I might never be able to work again . . . I have no friends or relations there. I didn't know what to think. I was very worried about my future.

One night I dreamed a wonderful dream. I had had many dreams since leaving Vietnam . . . some were nightmares, but this was quite different. I will never forget it as long as I live. I am sure God gave it to me, even though I did not really know Him well at this time.

In my dream, there was a man with a long, white robe, who spoke to me. He said, 'You must go to England, because there are many people there who will help you. You don't know any English but people will teach you there. You are ill but there is a way to be healed.'

Then many angels came to me and they were all dressed in white. Some gave me medicines; some taught me English. I was very happy and my dream seemed to go on all night. When I woke, I said, 'Oh, what a pity!' I was so sorry the dream was over, and yet it did not fade as dreams usually do. It stayed with me, growing stronger and stronger. At last I could stay in my bunk no longer. I had to get up and I walked all round the camp seven times. The camp was quite large, but I did not feel weak at all. My body seemed to be taken over by the Lord and I was not conscious of my paralysis. I felt completely well, and I was filled with a great happiness. I could hardly wait until morning to tell Noelle the news.

When I saw her, I tumbled all the words out to her and she was as glad as I was. She said, 'Yes, you remember that dream vividly. Don't let anyone take it from you! God gave you that dream to show you what you have to do next.'

After that, I had no doubts. I decided to go to England if they would have me. But I was sure they would; they would have to. It was in God's plan for my life. I withdrew my application to go to Canada and applied instead to go to England. The British authorities accepted me. But they wanted to know why I wanted to go to England. I didn't know what words to use to tell them that it was because I was believing in the Lord, so I said, 'I just want to go, that's all!'

The British authorities put a strong emphasis on education so they asked me what I did in Vietnam. I told them I was an interpreter between the Chinese and the Vietnamese, and they seemed pleased about this. They said, 'Good! We'll take you.'

Of course I still did not know what the future was to be in England but I felt sure I wouldn't starve. I was glad to be able to go.

May 1980 was the month set for my departure. I was excited and had no more fears. But the day before I was to leave for England, the doctor called me out of the queue and said, 'I'm sorry. You can't go. You are physically unfit to fly. Your heart is not good enough.'

I could not believe it. The shock and disappointment was too great. I had felt so much better since my dream and even my walking had improved. Nothing more had been said about an operation, though I still took medicine and saw the doctor regularly.

I had to stay behind again and see about seventy refugees off to England. Again I was alone. But, strangely, this time I did not feel quite so desolate. The Lord had given me a dream, and it was like a sign to me. I was sure I would go to England, but it was hard to wait. Noelle comforted me. She was sure I would go to England too.

The camp authorities took me to the hospital again and the doctor told me that I must undergo a small operation. He saw my distress and spoke to me kindly.

'Don't worry!' he said. 'It's a simple operation. We just want to patch you up so that you can travel by plane. Your heart has water in it and we must draw some off. This will help your heart to function properly. You will feel much stronger.'

I said, 'OK. I agree to have the operation.' I didn't really have much choice. I was not feeling too ill at this time, because I could walk a little, though my hand and arm were still useless.

'After the operation, your heart will be able to pump more efficiently and it will be quite safe for you to fly to England. I know it is hard to wait for the next plane-load of refugees, but the time will pass. You want to be well, don't you?'

He was quite right; I did want to be well. It was good of those doctors to look after my welfare. There were so many hundreds of refugees and yet the doctors made us feel we were important to *them* as well as to ourselves. I was grateful to them and I hope I was able to communicate this.

They all said that the operation was successful, and after one week I was able to leave hospital and return to Jubilee camp to wait for the next plane to England. I had to wait from May to September. It seemed like a very long time, but I was able to improve my walking and I went to as many of Noelle's Bible Studies as I could. I felt there was so much to learn. Perhaps there would be no opportunity for Christian teaching in England! Noelle was quite sure there would be, but I thought I would wait and see, and meanwhile I had a very old Chinese Bible. It had been given to me by one of the Chinese helpers on the camp. It was almost falling to pieces, but it was a great treasure to me. Noelle showed me where to begin reading.

When the plane arrived this time, I was allowed on board. I was glad to leave the crowded, dreary conditions of Jubilee camp, but I was sorry to leave Noelle and the other Christian missionaries, who had given me an eternal hope and some understanding of God's plan for my life. I would never forget the things that had happened to me in Hong Kong. I must have seen less of Hong Kong itself than any of the refugees, but I believed that I had gained more than any one from being there.

There were eighty-two of us refugees bound for England. The police called for me to do the interpreting because there were many who could not understand Cantonese. So I was made responsible for calling the roll. It was a good feeling to be working again. Perhaps there was still hope that I could be a translator in England?

When we reached London, we were all scattered . . . some to the north of England and some to the south. About thirty were sent to Sopley Reception Centre in Hampshire, and I was one of them.

6: England at last!

I can't remember very much about the coach journey from London Airport to Sopley. I know that as I climbed on to the bus full of refugees, the sun was shining and everywhere looked very peaceful. I had no interpreting to do. I was on my own. I think I dozed off to sleep. I had a safe, relaxed feeling that there was nothing more for me to do. The chatter went on around me. The children were quite enjoying the journey, though some were sick before we arrived. There was a policeman with us on the coach but he was not at all like our Vietnamese or Chinese policemen – he was so kind and gentle. He played with the children as if he were their father. I guessed that he probably had children of his own.

I wished that I understood English, but all I knew were the words 'Please' and 'Thank you' and 'OK' which everybody understood.

We stopped once at a large service station, where we could get drinks and use the wash rooms. There were crowds of English people there including a few black ones. They all stared at us, but they looked kind. We stared at them too; it was interesting. Altogether we were on the coach for about three hours.

It was not long after our stop when the driver called out, 'OK, this is Sopley!' These were the first words in English that I had really understood. I repeated them after him, and suddenly, all the refugees did the same. 'OK, Sopley!' they shouted.

The coach turned into some wide gates, with words

written in Vietnamese and Chinese as well as English. The first words we saw were: SOPLEY RECEPTION CENTRE. I sighed with relief. If the kind English people were going to write notices in our languages as well as their own, we should not feel so alien. There were also notices in the three languages about speed limits and other things.

Sopley was a large camp with a lot of huts scattered about. Best of all, it looked like home already, because there were hundreds of Vietnamese people milling about. They came running to the bus to welcome us all, smiling and laughing; there was a great deal of noise. The refugees looked well and happy. The sun was still shining and it was quite hot. We had expected it to be cold all the time. We shall be all right here, I said to myself. I caught sight of a large football field where boys were playing. It could almost have been Vietnam.

Then the thirty of us were led to a huge hut and again I felt isolated. Everyone had someone. If only I had just one of my own family! All the families were together. Then a small boy, who had sat beside me on the coach, came up to me and put his hand into my left one. (The right one was still useless!) He looked like my own son had looked once long ago.

'My mother's too busy looking after the babies,' he said. 'I'll stay with you.' This brought a warm feeling to my heart.

'OK, Phong,' I said, 'you look after me!' and we both laughed. We walked along to the registration hut together. It was like arriving in Hong Kong all over again. The English authorities had great notebooks which looked very official, but they could not manage our difficult names very well. When they called our names, we did not recognise them, unless the interpreters were there.

After a very long time, we were escorted to different huts. They all had numbers and mine was eleven. The huts were large enough to hold about twenty or twenty-five . . . one or two families. They did not know what to do with me as I did not fit into any family, but Phong hung on to my hand as if I were his uncle and so, for the first week or two, I stayed with his large family. At least we had all come all the way from Vietnam, so we had that in common. I had a tiny room to myself.

I sighed with relief as I put my few things into a drawer. I took out the Chinese New Testament that Noelle had got for me and read some verses. That made me feel really at home. It doesn't matter where I am, I thought to myself. God is everywhere. He will be looking after me here just as he did in Hong Kong.

But I wished Noelle could see me here in England. She was the one who first gave me the idea of coming and I knew she would be pleased. 'I am going to learn English very quickly,' I said aloud. There was no one to hear me. 'Then I shall write a letter to thank her.'

The dream was still lingering with me and in the quiet of the night I thought about those angels dressed in white. Perhaps I'll see one tomorrow, I thought. Perhaps they will begin to give me medicines and teach me English.

It was not long before I was called to the Sopley Hospital, and there were plenty of ladies dressed in white there; they took my temperature, tested my heart and pulse and gave me medicines. Then I was sent on to Boscombe Hospital. The doctor there looked grave.

'We must send you to Southampton Hospital,' he said kindly. We had an interpreter, so I was able to undersand what he was saying. 'You will need major heart surgery, but we are able to do it for you. Don't be afraid! You have an accumulation of fluid and this is why you are so tired all the time. If we give you a valve replacement, it will be like a life preserver. You will be strong again.'

'OK,' I said, smiling at him. They were all so kind and I was just a stranger. It really seemed they cared about me. 'I am not afraid,' I assured him.

It was true. I did not feel afraid this time, though I knew this was a serious operation, and the first one in Hong Kong had been only a small one. I wanted to be made completely better. I felt it was all part of God's plan for my life. I had been so sure that I would reach England safely and I now had hope for a good recovery.

I looked at the doctor. They had told me he was a heart specialist. Perhaps he is one of my angels, I said to myself. At least he is dressed in white!

I was beginning to think there must be many different kinds of angels. I was reading the gospel written by Luke. Noelle had told me that Luke was a doctor, so I enjoyed reading his account of Jesus's life. I particularly noticed all the references to angels in Luke's gospel.

There was an angel called Gabriel, who had come to tell Mary about the baby she was to have, who was to be called Jesus, because He was going to save people from their sins. Then another angel came to the shepherds to tell them that the baby who had just been born in a stable was the Saviour, Christ the Lord.

There were lots more angels in that story. Noelle had told me all about the first Christmas Day when God's Son was born. It must have been a happy day. I was looking forward to my first Christmas Day in England. But perhaps I would have to spend it in Southampton Hospital, not in the camp at Sopley. Wherever I am, I am sure the Lord will look after me, I said to myself. I belong to Him now.

Many wonderful things happened to me while I was in that hospital. These are the things I remember, more than the pain and the discomfort. I had many visitors. The friends I had made at Sopley came to see me.

'We are so sorry for you having to stay here so long,' they said. I replied, 'I would rather be here, safe and warm and with good food and drink than on that boat. *That* was too dangerous!' They all agreed with me. They had suffered too.

It was good to see people from my own country because it was so easy to talk and listen to them. I could understand a little English now but it was a strain and made me very tired. They told me that the operation had been a success and I thanked God for that, but they said I would feel very weak for a long time. I stayed in Southampton hospital for two whole months.

One of the nurses was a Chinese Christian and one of the doctors was too. There may have been more but these were the ones I knew. It was strange to me, but I could usually tell if someone was a Christian. Perhaps it was because they were interested in my Chinese New Testament, or perhaps the Christian family is like a normal family and you can recognise your own relations! They were concerned for me and they found a Chinese Christian man living in Southampton to visit me. His name was Lo.

We walked and talked. I had so many questions to ask and it was so easy to ask Lo in our own language. He spoke Cantonese as I did. Sometimes he would begin to answer before I had finished asking the question. We laughed a lot together. After Lo's first visit, I was quite exhausted, but very happy. I felt my Christian life had really begun. I did not know then that I was going to live in Southampton and meet this same Chinese Christian friend and go to his church. I just knew that the Lord was looking after me very specially.

The Head of the Sopley Camp came to see me too. That did surprise me and made me feel important. He really seemed to care about me.

One day I had another visitor. I had not met him before, but some of my friends had told me about him. He was an English man, a vicar, called Reverend Michael Meadows. He had lived in Vietnam for many years and his Cantonese was excellent. He was better than all the other interpreters because he was a Christian and could answer my questions about Christianity. We had a wonderful time together.

'I don't know what will happen to me when I come out of here,' I said to him, 'but I know the Lord will still go on looking after me.'

'That's right,' he agreed, 'and you'll be able to go to a Christian Church near Sopley.A coach goes there every Sunday and you will be able to understand because the service will be in English, Vietnamese and Chinese. You will be able to learn more about the Christian faith there.'

'Will there be Bible Study?' I asked. I could never forget Noelle's Bible Studies and what a help they had been to me.

'Oh yes,' Michael replied. 'There will be Bible Studies on the camp during the week.'

'Are there missionaries on the camp?' I asked. 'Are *you* a missionary?' and when he said he was, I grew very excited. I was beginning to see how God was leading me. My hope grew stronger and stronger as the days passed. My body grew stronger too. I was so happy that I longed to share my happiness with my countrymen who knew nothing of Jesus Christ and His power to save and heal. Perhaps *that* was part of the plan that God had for my life. Perhaps He would use me as a missionary! I was so glad I could speak both Chinese and Vietnamese.

First of all, I must learn more English. Living in England, I must know the language of the country. This thought made me eager to return to Sopley and start English lessons.

When I came out of hospital, I still felt very weak and much happier than when I was in Sopley before the operation. I had been assured that I could trust God with the whole of my life. Having that big operation was all part of the plan. The first part of my dream had already been fulfilled. There *were* people in England who could heal my body. And both English and Chinese people had ministered to my soul.

Now I was preparing for the second part. In my dream the man with the long robe had said to me, 'You do not know English but people will teach you there.'

My body was strong enough to take the teaching now. I had not yet met my teacher. I did so hope that she, too, would be a Christian. That would be like a double seal on my dream.

When the Sopley doctor thought I was strong enough for daily lessons, I was given the number of my classroom. It was A.16 and I was to have lessons in the afternoon only. I went along to the small room where the class was held. It was bright and cheerful and there were pictures and posters and maps all over the walls. We had a carpet on the floor and it was quite warm. There were about nine or ten students.

Although I had missed more than two months and the other students were far ahead of me, I felt full of hope. I was determined to study so hard that I would soon catch them up. I had never really worried about learning the language. I had picked up French very easily.

What I had forgotten was that our teachers of French were Chinese speaking. They could explain the difficult words in our own language. My English teacher's name was Frida and she did not know one word of Chinese. So I had to learn English in English.

I looked at the teacher. She did not seem like an angel at all, at least not like the angels in my dream. She was dressed in pink, not white, and she laughed a lot. That did not mean she was not a Christian, of course. The American missionaries laughed too. And Lo and I had laughed together in the hospital.

Teacher Frida enjoyed teaching us, I could tell that, but she was hopeless at my language. Even the numbers up to ten sounded dreadful when she proudly attempted to say them. We all laughed at her and she did not mind a bit. In fact, all our English lessons were fun.

This worried me at first because I wanted so much to learn, and I thought we should be more serious. After a few days, however, I discovered that I was learning new words fast. But I was so impatient to learn more about

God, and instead we had to learn to speak proper English!

One day I knew that I had to ask Teacher Frida if she was a Christian. I suspected that she was, but I had waited until I was more sure. I should be so disappointed if the answer was ‘no’. So I waited until the end of the English lesson and said in my best English, ‘Teacher Frida, are you Christian?’

I knew that I had got the words right, but she looked so surprised at first. I think she was amazed to hear me say the word ‘Christian’. Then she nearly knocked me over! I was not holding on to anything and my legs were not strong. She shook both my hands and told me I was her brother in the Lord. I felt glad and told her she was my brother too!

Oh, I did wish that I knew more English, but Teacher Frida went on talking for a long time without words and I understood her. She used signs like deaf and dumb people do. I knew she was saying that we were both in the same family . . . God’s family, and that I need not feel alone. I should have liked to have told her about the dream, but I did not have the words then. I would be able to tell her later, when I had learnt the word ‘angel’ in English!

7: Life at Sopley

I continued to enjoy my English lessons, although they were hard work. Frida used to insist on our listening and speaking the words before writing anything down; and we did not like this at first. It was hard to remember words unless we wrote them down.

Ban was one who went his own way. He refused to listen first, so that although he was quicker at learning than the rest of us and could write things correctly, his spoken English was terrible. Teacher Frida used to get cross with him. 'Pen down, Ban!' she would say, as he tried to cover up what he was doing.

She had rather a clever way of catching us out. She would sit down with her back to us and one by one we had to say a word or sentence in English. These were always words that we knew well.

'If *I* can't tell what you are saying,' she told us, 'no one will. I am used to you and can guess what you are trying to say. If I look at your faces I can understand, but other people will not understand at all.'

Ban was very bad at doing this, but still he tried to write more than listen. Ha was the quickest of us all. He tried both to write and speak well and he was the only one of us who succeeded.

Ha was a rather comical young man who used to call Teacher Frida 'Mum'. I think she liked it. She had told us that she had no children. One day, Ha knocked out one of his front teeth and had to stay away. Frida asked, 'Where is Ha today?' His sister Lien replied, 'He has got a window in his mouse.' (She was one of those who could not pronounce 'th'!) Three days later, Ha was absent again. 'Has Ha got another window in his mouth?' asked Frida, laughing. 'No,' replied Lien. 'He has gone to have his window shut!'

Lien was very quick too but she never managed to master the 'th' sound all the time she was at Sopley. (I could just manage it, though it was difficult at first.) I remember one day when we were learning about the parts of our bodies, and answering questions with different numbers. Frida would ask, 'How many eyes have you got?' and we had to reply, 'I have two eyes.' At last she asked Lien, 'How many thumbs have you got?' and Lien replied, 'I have two *tums*' When Lien was resettled in her new home she wrote letters to all of us and she signed her name to Teacher Frida 'your student Tums!'

We spent two hours every afternoon on our English lessons but this was not all. At four o'clock every day we had to go to the Red Room . . . a huge room where we had films and talks on various subjects. The speakers talked in English and we had Vietnamese and Chinese interpreters.

'You must go to these lessons,' our teachers told us over and over. 'It is a requirement of the Home Office.'

Although some of the subjects were interesting, none of us liked going to the Red Room. We had talks and films about the National Health Service, first aid, sanitation, money, customs, banks and religion. The teachers did not know what they had to do to make us go. They came with us to the doors, they sat with us, but even then many of the young men escaped. Ha and Ban used to creep out of the windows!

The main reason why we disliked these sessions was that we were too tired to take a third hour after our long English lesson. And the women did not want to go because it was cooking time. We always had our big meal in the evening, when we had rice and meat or shellfish and garlic and onions. We ate in our own huts where we slept, but the cooking and washing went on in other huts opposite our living huts. We had a number of toilets and wash basins in our sleeping huts too.

One day Teacher Frida took us in the mini-bus to a small town called New Milton, where we were to visit a bank. The interpreter had explained it to us before we left Sopley and she came with us, but we had still not really understood. It was called Lloyds Bank and Teacher Frida told us that all her money was there.

I did not understand why we had to visit a bank, as we had no money to put in or draw out. 'You may have some one day,' Frida told us, 'and then you will want to know what to do.'

She picked out Ban and gave him something to do to try out his English. He was very confident. Frida showed him how to write a cheque to take out five pounds in cash.

'Hand it over the counter,' she told him. 'Then he will say to you, 'How d'you want it?'

'What shall I say?' asked Ban.

'Say, 'I'll have five one pound notes please!''

Ban practised saying it first, and I thought it sounded quite good. We all tried it. Then Ban handed the cheque over to the man, who was called a bank clerk. The man said to him, 'How will you have it?' and although that was a different question, Ban said very loudly 'I'll have five one pound notes, please!'

Teacher Frida looked proud. I watched her face. But the bank man said, 'Pardon?' Poor Ban had to say the sentence three times altogether. He did not look quite as confident after that. I wondered if now he would listen more than write!

On our next English lesson we did a great deal of writing and Ban was happy. We wrote words like 'account', 'deposit', 'cheque-book', 'withdraw', 'manager', 'clerk'.

We went on a number of visits as the weather grew warmer again. We enjoyed England when the sun shone: Sopley Camp looked quite pretty then. There were a lot of trees around and the leaves were beginning to put out shoots. It was not far to the river. The children found it too cold for paddling in early spring, but the teachers told them it would warm up in the summer. The men and boys played football but just as the weather began to be really pleasant, they gave up football and started playing cricket instead.

'Why?' we asked. 'Why do you only play football when the weather is so bad? The summer is the best time to play.'

'No, we only play during the football season,' one of the field-workers told us, 'and the season is winter.'

It did not seem very sensible, as for so many weeks in the winter it was impossible to play anything out of doors at all. We played all the year round in Vietnam.

There were always ping-pong games in the Hall. Some of the teachers were surprised at our skill. I only wished *I* could play. I had been very skilful once! Still, I watched the games and sometimes scored for the players. We had to score in English. The teachers often played with us and my teacher, Frida, was very keen on playing, which was surprising because she was fairly old. She had told us she was the oldest teacher at Sopley.

'I want to play your champion,' she said, 'but he will have to play with his left hand only.' We often used to do this when playing with the children. It gave them a better game.

Frida did play Quang, who was our Number One player. She won too! I think he let her win – he was very fast, even when using only his left hand.

We used to visit various second-hand shops in Boscombe and in Southampton. We went on the mini-bus and everyone wanted to go on these trips. Sometimes a man would hide his son and smuggle him into the bus when the teacher was not looking. This always made our teachers cross, although we could not think why they should be. If there was room, and a boy needed some more shoes, it seemed sensible to fill the bus. It was probably something to do with the Home Office. Whenever there was something we could not understand, it was always to do with the Home Office. Yet when the men came from the Home Office, they were very friendly and talked to us kindly.

At the second-hand shops we bought suitcases to hold our belongings when we were resettled, and household things like mincers, saucepans, plates and cups which were very cheap in those shops. We had to think forward to the things we should need in our new homes.

One day Teacher Frida told us that the next day we were going to have the mini-bus and go for a visit to the New Forest. The weather was bright and sunny, though we still had to wear our coats.

'Be here by 1.30 p.m.' she told us. 'Don't be late! We will have a nice time.'

We were all afraid. 'Forest' was a frightening word to us. I had had quite enough of forests to last me the rest of my life, so I was determined not to go. Besides, I was not really strong enough yet. 'We are not going either,' said all the others, but they did not tell the teacher. She would not understand.

So no one turned up at the mini-bus.

The next day we all arrived at our classroom as usual. Teacher Frida was very disappointed with us. She said,'Why? Why did you not come? You are a good class for coming to English lessons and some of you are even good about coming to the Red Room lessons. This was a treat for you. I had to book the bus a whole week in advance.'

We could not explain. We just said, 'Teacher Frida, we're very sorry. We're very bad students. We will work hard now.' We did not make excuses. We knew she would not understand.

'What does 'booking' a mini-bus mean?' I asked and Frida explained it to us clearly. 'You have to book a holiday before you go,' she said, 'and you can book a seat on the train to London before you travel. You can buy your ticket weeks before you travel. With the minibus there are all the classes wanting it at once, so you have to sign your name on a list. That is what 'booking it' means.

'And here is my *book*,' said Linh.

We were learning that there were many English words that sounded like each other and were even spelt like each other but meant different things. The word 'LIGHT' was like this. It took us a long time to say it properly, though we could write it and spell it easily. First we used to say 'ligh'. (It is not easy for us to sound the last letter.) Then when we tried to copy the teacher, watching her mouth as she said it, we came out with 'lighter'. It sounded to us as though she had sounded the last letter like that. We had to learn to *say* 'ligh' loudly, and then*whisper* the -t. Then it came out light 'light'. It was the same with 'night' and 'bright'.

We had difficulties with other words like this. One of the men teacher's names was Nick! And another teacher was Pat. We learnt to be more careful.

Of course we all knew what 'light' meant. That was easy. There was the light up on the ceiling. The sun gave light. We switched on the light. But one day our teacher brought some things for us to look at and hold. 'These are heavy,' she said. 'These are light.' We were surprised. Here was a new meaning for 'light'. A tissue was light . . . a pile of books was heavy.

'People are heavy,' said Ban, trying to be clever.

'Some of them are,' said Frida. She fetched one of the children from the first school. She was Kieu's little girl, and she was five years old and very tiny. 'Now Ban,' she said laughing, 'pick up little Hoa and then pick up Cuong.' (He was the biggest of us all!)

'OK, OK' he said. 'Hoa is light. Cuong is heavy. But if I hold Hoa and then a tissue, *she* is heavy and the tissue is light.'

We all clapped. We could not help liking Ban though he did show off a lot!

We all thought teacher Frida had forgotten about the forest, so we came along to lessons quite happily every day. Then one Friday, the interpreter came up to the classroom, which was something that did not happen very often. She explained to us what the teacher was saying. We *were* going to the New Forest, and this time everyone was going. She explained that it was not optional. We had to go; it was part of our English course. We understood that all right. Ha began looking at the windows. I told the interpreter to tell the teacher that I was not well enough to go to the forest. That was where I had become ill, and I was only just better. We all looked solemn.

Then the teacher said no more, and the Chinese interpreter talked to us. She explained there was nothing at all to be afraid of. The New Forest was nothing like the New Economic Zones, to which we were so terrified of being sent in Vietnam. She had been many times and it was quite different. She showed us photographs of herself with a Chinese family and there were pictures of tame ponies and little streams and lightly forested woods. They did not look dark at all, and the ground was soft and flat. She showed us pictures of some of the Vietnamese families, and they all looked happy.

We began to feel better about going. In any case, it looked as if we *had* to go. There was even another teacher going with us. The interpreter came with us right up to the door of the mini-bus. No one escaped, not even Ha. One of the men from another class came running up and asked if he could go too. He liked it in the Forest. That made us feel much happier.

'What's it like?' we asked him, even though the interpreter had told us already. We knew she had only told us what the teacher had told her to say. 'You are lucky to go,' he said. 'It's like a holiday.' But they would not let him come with us. This was for our class only.

'When did you book the mini-bus?' I asked and Frida said, 'Oh good, you have remembered! I booked it last week when you were all so bad and did not come.'

'Oh sorry, teacher!' we all said again and this time we laughed. We were not afraid any more. Without the interpreter we should never have understood. Without her, I don't think the teacher would have understood either.'

The New Forest was beautiful. The sun was shining and the light was slanting through the great trees. We could see the sky through the trees and it was blue; there were no clouds at all. We did not feel shut in. I thought of my sister Thu Thuy, thousands of miles away in Canada. She would love this forest. She would write a poem about it. But I knew there were many forests in Canada. I hoped my family were all happy wherever they were. In the letters they had written to me they all sounded well and happy.

There were hundreds of ponies. They did not seem to belong to anyone. They were so tame that they came right up to us but there was an English law that said we must not feed them, because they fed on the grass. Frida explained about the penalty if anyone was seen feeding the animals. (Penalty was a new word to us but it was easy to understand.)

'If you feed the ponies near the bus or a car,' she said, 'they will walk across the road when they see cars coming and they could be run over or cause an accident.'

I really enjoyed walking about in the forest. We left the mini-bus and just wandered about in the open; it was more like large fields than a forest. We learnt the word 'country', the opposite of 'town'. Most of us liked the towns best, but it was very peaceful in the country. You could go slowly and look at more things. I think it suited me just then because I did not want to walk very fast. I still limped, but I felt I was growing stronger every day.

'It is not like forest land at all,' I told the two teachers. I tried to explain to them, in English, about the forest land between Vietnam and China, where I had pushed through the rough under and overgrowth and splashed through the muddy rivers and swamps. I told them about the poisonous snakes and the terrible insects and the steep rugged mountains.

I was the only one in the class who had worked in those forests, but all our people dreaded the thought of being sent to the New Economic Zones. These were thousands of miles of polluted land, ruined by the war bombs and the chemical bombs and land mines that covered the area; rubber plantations were destroyed and miles of timber lay useless. This had all been done to stop the enemy making use of the assets that South Vietnam had to offer. While we were still in Vietnam, we had been told that it would take many, many years of hard labour to restore our land. There were some six of these zones in the North too, and it was the rich middle class people who used to be sent there. All our people dreaded this as much as a concentration camp.

Later, back in the camp, I told the interpreter all about them, and she passed it on to the teachers. They both went very quiet. I think they understood why we had refused to go to the New Forest that first time. We felt we had been silly but now we realised that the New Forest was nothing like we had feared. We had expected the ground to be full of large dangerous holes, like the craters on the moon, that you see on TV.

Ban said, 'Please, may we go again? We like *your* forest.' 'Perhaps,' replied our teacher, 'but remember, I have to book in advance.'

We did not take books or pens out on our visits, except when we went to Lloyds Bank, but we were learning all the time.

'This is as good as an English lesson,' said Cuong on one visit.

'It *is* an English lesson,' replied Frida.

Among some of the classes that were given in the Red Room were those for mothers and babies. The Vietnamese mothers did not like these because they thought they knew all there was to know about bringing up babies. After all, they had a lot of experience.

Later, they came to realise that there were many things they needed to know before they could get what they wanted in the shops or from the Health Centre. They began to see that the English teachers were not trying to stop them from being Vietnamese. They wanted to help them to live more easily in a different sort of country.

They even taught us their National Anthem, 'God Save The Queen'. We grew so used to it that Frida had only to play one chord and we would all stand to attention. We have grown quite patriotic about Great Britain and its Queen. After all, she and her Government allowed us to escape and live in her country. We enjoyed seeing pictures of British Royalty. My favourites were Prince Charles and Princess Diana. Most of the English people seem to like them too.

We tried to teach our teachers some of our special Vietnamese songs. Ly duc Minh played the guitar and sang very well and we all grew sad and happy at once while his songs took us back to our past. When you have left your own land, you don't want to forget the old poems and songs, though they make you ache inside. I thought for the first time that I really understood my sister Thu Thuy more than I had ever done. If she had been here with me, she would be writing a lot of poems. I kept thinking of her and wondering whether she was happy in Canada.

The English teachers were very interested in our Chinese New Year celebrations. They gave us some days free from lessons so that we could carry on our festivities. On New Year's Eve we used to worship our ancestors and gods. I knew that I should not be doing that any more. I had one God now, and He was the only one I should worship. But it was a good chance to invite the teachers and my new Christian friends to my hut. Mr. Hicks, from Hurn Christian Fellowship Church, and his wife had already been to see me in Sopley, and we had prayed together. We had shared their Christmas festival and their New Year, and now they were willing to share ours.

But somehow the celebration was not the same in Sopley. The English wanted us to hold on to our traditions and were very helpful. They supplied us with hundreds of chickens for our feasts, and we had a huge dragon walk as we had in Vietnam. But it almost seemed as if the English people were more interested in our dragon walk than we were ourselves. When the walk began around the camp most of the refugees were inside their huts. This would never have happened in Vietnam.

Perhaps we had had too many holidays all at once! There was the English Christmas, which was very colourful and exciting, with presents and cards for us all and good food. The whole camp was decorated. And then, almost immediately, came *their* New Year, although apart from a few people who came from Scotland, there was not so much excitement then. Then on February 5th came our Chinese New Year.

'Tet' was our word for the New Year Festival, and this year, 1981 was called the Year of the Chicken. Even if it was not quite as it would have been at home, the refugees tidied up and dressed up for the occasion and made the camp look as beautiful as possible. All the families were busy making special cakes called 'Banh Day' and 'Banh Chung' . . . representing the Sun and the Earth. Some of the women wore traditional dress that they had made themselves in the sewing room at Sopley. Teacher Frida took photographs of Kieu and Lien from our class. 'Oh, you do look beautiful,' she said.

'I keep thinking back to last New Year,' said the father of little Phong, who still looked upon me as his uncle. 'It is so different here.'

'We are safe here,' 'I reminded him, and we have freedom.'

'But what is the use of freedom if we have no security for the future, no resettlement yet, no jobs? The English people themselves cannot get jobs!'

This was true. Unemployment was constantly talked about by our teachers, our administrators and cooks.

'Cooks will always be wanted,' I said, smiling. 'Our cooking is good.'

We all learnt cooking and the English teachers liked us to teach them too. Before very long they were all using chop sticks; that is, all except Frida. She could not use them at all. We all tried very hard to teach her but she could not pick up even one piece of chicken.

'I think there is something wrong with my fingers,' she said seriously, but we all laughed at her.

'Perhaps you are too old to learn' I said to her to make her feel better, but she did not seem to feel any better because of that.

After all, Teacher Frida had taught one Vietnamese lady to write, who was quite old, at least sixty, and she had never held a pen in her hand before. She had never been to school. I am sure that must have been harder than learning to use chopsticks. But Frida could not do it and after a while she gave up trying. We all used to give her a fork when she came to meals in our huts.

We loved having our teachers for meals with us. We liked them all very much and they took a great deal of trouble to help us with books and dictionaries. There was one man in our group who had driven a car and a lorry back in Vietnam, and he asked Frida to help him fill in an application form for driving in England. Even when we understood the words on the forms and the interpreters were with us, they still did not seem to make sense. We spent a lot of time learning to fill in different kinds of forms, especially medical ones. I thought that was very useful.

We learnt the words for different parts of cars too, though I was quite sure I would never be able to drive one. When I thought of myself as a young man roaring along the roads to Hanoi on my motor-bike, I felt very sad. And when I saw the rest of the class making boats and baskets in the art and craft lessons, I was sad again, for my right arm and hand were still useless. But it was not right to feel too miserable about this, because I was growing clever with my left hand, and my brain still felt very alert. Besides, I knew that I had something far more wonderful than a strong right arm. I had a real Friend, who held me by my hand and led me along. Jesus would never let me go; I belonged to Him and every day I was learning more about Him.

Many of our people made hammocks, which they used all the time for their babies. Apparently the English people wanted them too. I'm not sure why they wanted them, because they did not sleep in them or use them for their children, but it was a good chance for the Vietnamese to make a little money. Some of my friends gave Teacher Pat a hammock and two model boats for her own boys. Her name was one that we found difficult to say. We had the word 'phat' in our language, which we pronounced 'fat', so we called our teacher 'Fat File', because her family name was Pile.

'That's all right,' she told us, 'as long as you don't call me 'Fat Fool''

We all laughed with her because we could see she wanted us to, but we had no idea why it was funny. Then one day Kin explained to us what a fool was and we were very amused!

Teacher Pat was a very popular teacher. She always went to every Chinese meal that was going. She loved our food, but Teacher Frida didn't. *She* used to drink a lot of Chinese tea!

On December 16th 198O we visited Teacher Frida in her home. I never forget the date because she made us all write our names and addresses in a book, which she said was called a Visitor's Book. She lived in a bungalow by the sea. All our English group went and we had cups of tea or coffee and different kinds of biscuits. Frida invited some of her English friends and we had to open the door to them and invite them in. Then we handed round the food. It was good practice. We had to say, 'Would you like a piece of cake? . . . Do you like tea or coffee?'

Teacher Frida had a large white dog called Misty, who she said was a guard dog. We had guard dogs in Vietnam before 1954, but not as pets. If they bit anyone, they had to be killed at once: we were so afraid of rabies. The Vietnamese used to breed dogs and cats for food. Some people liked dog meat very much.

But Misty did not seem like a guard dog at all, though he barked loudly when the door bell rang. The women were afraid, but they did not see his tail wagging at the other end!

'I don't think he is a very good guard dog,' I told Frida.

'He's beautiful,' she replied, so perhaps I had got the English words wrong. But he would let robbers in, I thought to myself. He would not even bite a thief. I did not say this out loud because we could see that Frida really thought of her dog as a companion . . . not a guard! He was far too friendly.

'He *is* a very good guard dog,' she persisted. We wondered if perhaps he was such a clever animal, he could tell at once whether someone was a thief or a bad person!

'He thinks we are all good people,' said Ha. 'He would always let *us* in.'

'You are all good,' Frida replied, laughing. That was one of our English jokes. In A.16 one of our lessons went like this!

'I'm good. You're good. He's good. We're good. We're *all* good.' Then we learnt to ask the questions of each other.

'Are you good, Sang?' 'Yes, I'm good,' I would answer.

'Are you good, Lien?' 'Yes, I'm good.'

'Are you good, Ha?' 'No, I'm not good!' he would answer, and he was right. He was not good but we all liked him, because he was so jolly. He was always late for lessons and sometimes he didn't come at all.

I never wanted to miss lessons. I *had to* learn to speak good English for I believed that my mastering English was all part of God's plan for my life and I had to play my part. I had no idea how wonderfully He was going to take over my life for me.

It had not been very long after my return from Southampton Hospital when I had found myself in a large coach on my way to Hurn Christian Fellowship Church. This coach came every Sunday to the gates of Sopley Camp and people used to crowd in and fill every seat . . . men, women and many children. The first time I went along, I felt thrilled to know that so many Vietnamese people wanted to hear the gospel. I suppose this would have been called a Tinlanh Church in our homeland.

The building was right in the New Forest. There was no need to be afraid of the New Forest ever again! It was quite a small church but the Bible text outside the door was the biggest message there could be. There were three words over the door . . . GOD IS LOVE. I *knew* this was true.

I shall never forget my first visit there. We had a huge, warm welcome from the preacher, the Reverend Roy Hicks, and the singing of the hymns and choruses made me think about Heaven for the first time. Mr Meadows, whom I had met in the hospital, was there; he had come to interpret. One or two of the teachers from the camp were there, but I was disappointed that my teacher was not there. She had told me she went to another church where she taught children, but she did come to Hurn once or twice. Mr Meadows interpreted for the Chinese speaking people and he was very good at it. He was as good as a Cantonese speaker, and so was his wife.

It was the first time I had sung to God in my own language. Although I was so happy, it made me want to cry. The children sang and laughed and clapped their hands. I clapped with my heart instead of my hands! At that church, I began to understand a little more of the Christian faith. It was put to us very simply, but I had a feeling there was much more to know.

There was such an abundance of love shown at Hurn Church! I called it 'unconditional love', for there were no strings attached. I was able to love God there and worship Him with many other Christians and I began to read and understand my Chinese Bible. It was a very, very old Bible, almost falling to pieces. I did not mind its age: it was not as old as the story of Jesus. Having the whole Bible, as well as a New Testament, was a great help to me and I spent many hours in my hut studying it. If I had a difficult question I could ask Mr Meadows or Mr Hicks.

'Come along to the Bible Study tonight, Sang,' Samuel said to me one day after lessons. He was a Chinese young man who was staying on the camp to help us.

'Oh yes,' I replied eagerly. It was just what I wanted. 'Where is it and what time?' I would not miss this for the world. I thought again of Noelle and her Bible Studies on the Parables of Jesus.

After that, I went along to the Bible Studies every week. They were held on the camp in Sopley and although we did sing some hymns and choruses, most of the time was given to reading and learning about the Bible. I learnt that as well as believing Jesus, I needed to confess Him to my friends. This was new to me but I could see at once that it was right. How could I keep the Good News to myself? It had to be shared. Every single person I knew needed salvation desperately.

'My friends won't come to hear for themselves,' I said, 'so I shall have to take the message to them. If Noelle had not brought the message to me in Hong Kong, I might never have heard it at all.'

'That's right,' said Samuel. 'The disciple Andrew was really the first Christian missionary we read of in the Bible, for he brought his brother Simon Peter to Jesus.'

That made me feel sad. ‘My brothers are all far away,’ I said to him. ‘I can’t bring them.’

‘No, but you can pray for them,’ he told me, ‘and you can tell your friends here how the Lord Jesus has saved you and brought you into His family.’

‘Perhaps I could tell them all in Hurn Church,’ I said. ‘I’d like to do that. People give testimonies every week. Do you think I could?’

‘I’m sure you could. I’ll speak to the minister. But it is harder to speak here in the camp and in your classroom than in a church where everyone wants to learn about God. You try here first!’

It was good advice and I took it. I did find it hard to talk to my Vietnamese friends on the camp. They were always going off somewhere else. There were many films showing in the cinema and whole families used to go there in the evenings. There always seemed to be something special happening like a football match or a film just when we had Bible Studies.

There were children’s meetings on the camp every week and I used to go to those as well. Although I had no children to take myself, I liked to look at their faces as they sang and played games and asked questions. The stories were very well told by Karen, who worked in the Office. She seemed to understand the children. Someone told me she had not been a Christian for very long, but she did know the Bible well. I wished I could tell the Bible stories as well as she did.

Sometimes they would ask me to help with the interpreting from Vietnamese to Chinese and then I felt really happy. This was something I *could* do. It did not need my right hand and arm. I felt I was being useful again and doing something I longed to do. I wondered if God could still use my talent as an interpreter!

There was one chorus we learnt to sing in English at the Bible Study evening at Sopley, which I liked very much.

I know who holds the future, and He'll guide me
with His hand,
With God things don't just happen; everything by
Him is planned;
So as I face tomorrow with its problems large
and small;
I'll trust the God of miracles; give to Him my all.

I knew that God worked miracles today as in the days of the Bible, and I thought He had already worked one in my life. I knew He still had a plan for me, and that I could rely on Him.

8 Southampton

'Phung Ngoc Sang! Come to the Office please!'

The tannoy system was always busy on the camp at Sopley. People were being called all day long, but it was exciting to hear your own name. You never knew what it might be about.

'Phung Ngoc Sang! Come to the Office please!'

It sounded urgent. Perhaps it was to do with my resettlement! I must hurry. Although I was feeling nearly well now and had been five months in Sopley since my operation, it was difficult for me to hurry. My heart was better but my leg still dragged and my right arm was useless.

'Phung Ngoc Sang! Phung Ngoc Sang!'

I was on my way now. It was a Saturday and the children were running around, for there was no school that day. Little Phong had heard the message and came running to tell me. He walked along beside me. He and his family were being resettled in Bristol the next day and maybe I should not see them again. Most of the Vietnamese who had come from Hong Kong with me on the plane had already gone to other places. I think I had been a problem, because I still needed to be looked after.

In the Resettlement Office, I found two people, Mr Meadows and a tall girl called Valerie who worked there. I knew she had tried very hard to find a place for me to live. She was looking happy . . . almost excited. My heart began to beat faster.

'We have good news for you, Sang,' she said. 'There is a house in Southampton called 'Bethany House' and there is room for you there.'

I sat down rather suddenly. It was a shock but a very pleasant one. 'Southampton?' I said. 'That is wonderful!'

When I had thought about the future, I always had hope in my heart that I should be resettled somewhere near some Chinese Christians. There were many in Southampton; I knew this already. I had met some of them while I was in the hospital. I thought of Lo and the happy talks we had had together. He had told me about a Chinese Church nearby. Was *this* how the Lord was answering my prayers? Or was this what He had in mind for me all along?

Suddenly I realised that Valerie was talking all about my new home and I had heard nothing. But it didn't really matter to me. My God *was* the God of miracles and I knew I could trust Him for my future. But I must be grateful to these kind people too, because I believed that God was using them to carry out His plan.

'Thank you very much,' I said. 'It is very, very good news. I am happy.'

And then I did listen, and I learnt all about my new home in England. Mr Meadows was translating what Valerie said so I could understand it all clearly.

Bethany was a big house that used to be owned by the nuns at the convent just across the road from it. It was opened in 1903 for women and girls who had problems. Now a Mr Carr-Gomm had bought it for lonely, single people and I was to be the first resident. I would have a small room all to myself and Jill, the housekeeper, would see that I was all right, and give me one big meal each evening. I could boil kettles for myself and make tea or coffee when I wanted it. Soon there would be other residents, so I would not be lonely.

I knew Jill, because she had a boy friend on the Camp. He was one of our fieldworkers and both he and Jill were Christians.

'And you will have time to study and a room to yourself,' Mr Meadows said. I was glad about that.

The first few days at Bethany House were a bit confusing for me, though I knew everything would be all right. God was in control of my life. But unless Mr Meadows was there to translate for me, I still had problems with my English. People at Sopley and at Hurn Fellowship had grown used to my kind of English, but when I went into the shops it was not so easy. I said the right words, but it must had *sounded* wrong. Jill was very kind to me but she could not understand me at all; I was glad Valerie came with me on that first day. She was like part of Sopley. So many people came to see me. Sister Elizabeth came from the Convent . . . a very good lady, but we could not communicate. Mr. Carr-Gomm came too, and they all talked a lot. They smiled at me a lot too. I smiled back because that was the one way we could communicate.

The house was comfortable and large. There were nine small bedrooms, a pleasant lounge where we could sit together, bathrooms and a utility room.

My room was upstairs. When I went up there and shut my door and took out my Bible, I felt at home. I spread my bedcover over my bed, hung up my family pictures and put my few possessions in the drawers.

Soon the second resident arrived. His name was Jimmy and, like me, he was all alone in the world. He was an Englishman. We talked together a little, and we laughed a lot.

Mr Meadows visited me, and Mr and Mrs Hicks from the Hurn Christian Church, and then one day, my Chinese friend, Lo, came to see me. From then, things began to move fast. I went along to the Chinese Church and met many new Christian friends. It was so good to be able to understand and be understood. Best of all, I began to learn more about my Lord. The Bible was making more sense to me. It was God's Word and I wanted to follow its words.

By the time that Bethany had filled all its places with nine residents and Jill, the housekeeper, had left for another place, I was feeling really at home. My room was very comfortable. I had a fish tank full of coloured tropical fish, and I loved to see them slipping through the water. They were so beautiful. *They* were God's creatures too.

The new housekeeper was young and her name was Julie; her mother had helped in the Bethany house too. They were both Christians and once or twice I went along with Julie to her church. It was a happy, welcoming place and everyone was kind to me. They tried to make me understand and feel at home, but still the language was a barrier. I was sure I would be better off at the Chinese Church.

Well, those early days are over now and I have been at Bethany for nearly two years, but I have not forgotten my own country.

Every time I use my bamboo chop-sticks I think back to the bamboo plantations in the mountains where the wild animals were so dangerous. One day in Southampton, Julie gave us a new vegetable with a strange name.

'What is it?' I asked her. 'It tastes like bamboo shoots.'

'No, it is asparagus,' she told me. 'Do you like bamboo shoots?' And then I told her all about the different uses we make of bamboo; how the important people like to grow them in their gardens as an ornament; how they are planted in the mountains to discourage tigers and made into flutes for playing; how the merchants in Hong Kong buy them from the Vietnamese and make garden seats and fences and baskets.

'It is a valuable plant' I told her, 'and the edible shoots are very expensive. We used to buy them before the Communists came.'

'Whatever was that about tigers?' Julie asked.

'Oh, there were lots of tigers in North Vietnam, and when I worked in the mountains between Vietnam and China they were one of our great enemies. The bamboo grows so thick and close together that even tigers can't break through them.'

'I've always liked tigers,' Julie admitted, 'but of course I've only seen them behind bars. They are beautiful animals.'

I still make many mistakes in my English. Only today I was working with Julie on an exercise in my book. I do a great deal of homework. It was the story of a little girl called Jane. I wrote down that Jane had hurt her *uncle*.

'No, no,' said Julie, 'the word is 'ankle', not 'uncle'.' She had to explain it to me by showing me her ankle! So many words are difficult even now. Yesterday I met the words 'passing by.'

'You can use the word 'pass' in so many ways,' I said. 'You talk of passing *in* the door . . . or passing *away*, to mean dying. That's not the same thing at all. Then you pass the butter down the table, passing *down*. Are there any more?'

Julie opened her eyes wide at this. 'That is very clever of you, Sang,' she said, 'you are working it out for yourself. Good! Keep it up!'

'*Are* there any more?' I asked again.

'You pass an exam,' Julie said.

'And you pass by on the other side,' I said laughing. I had just been reading the story of the Good Samaritan.

'Very good,' said Julie. 'Shall I give you a very hard one to think about? 'Passing the buck' means to hand something on to someone else . . . something you don't want yourself.'

After thinking for a long time, I said, 'Yes, I've got it,' and I really thought I had. Next day, after breakfast, it was my turn on the rota to do the washing-up with Frank, so I picked up the tea-towel and gave it to Julie and said, 'I am passing you the back.'

Everybody at the table laughed and laughed.

'Buck, Sang!' said Julie. 'You have the idea all right, but you got the word wrong. It's 'passing the buck'. But that was a good try. As a reward, I *will* do your washing-up for your today.'

And she did. I don't think I shall ever forget that word again.

I have grown quite used to English food. I enjoy roast lamb with green peas and mint sauce. Best of all I like hot beef with the vegetables that are like tiny little cabbages but are called sprouts. There is another meal we have that Julie makes with cheese. I made a mistake with this the other day: I thought it was called 'Cheesey-flowers'. The vegetables do look like little flowers made of cheese, but they are called cauliflowers! I often wonder if I shall ever know all the names properly.

I have a very good teacher of English, who comes to me every Tuesday. He sets me homework too and my writing book fills up very quickly. But it is impossible for him to teach me all I need to know. Lately, I have been having extra lessons three times a week, but to get to these I have to walk for forty minutes, and then it is forty minutes back again. I thank God that I am able to do all this walking and studying. Before the operation on my heart, this would not have been possible.

It isn't just the language that is difficult. There are many other things that are so different from Vietnam. When I went to Peking I thought things were very different there, but the basic way of life was the same; In England, I have had to learn that the Eastern and Western cultures are sometimes almost opposite.

I will give an example. I am extremely grateful to the British people for permitting me to live in England, and to the Resettlement officials who found a place for me at Bethany House; to Noelle, Mr Meadows, Mr Hicks and the Chinese Church for the spiritual help they have all given, and for all the other kind people who have helped me in any way at all. But I do not keep saying 'thank you' all the time. I find that the English are always saying it. Saying it once is not enough.

In a shop, the English will buy the goods and hand

over the money, so they have a right to the things they have bought. Yet still they say, ‘Thank you very much. Thank you. Good morning. Thank you,’ and then the man who has sold them the things says ‘thank you’ as well. I don’t know why *he* has to say ‘thank you’. Perhaps he is glad to have the custom.

In Vietnam, if a mother asks her child to move something for her or fetch a chair, she will not thank her for doing it. She will just expect her to do it. In England, it seems that whatever you do, child or adult, you must use the words ‘thank you’ and ‘please’. In Vietnam, people who are close to us, family or friends, do not expect thanks. This would mean they were not real friends.

Then there’s the weather. One Englishman will say, ‘It’s not so cold today, is it?’ and the other man will answer, ‘No, but I think the wind’s freshening up, don’t you?’ and the first man replies ‘Ah, perhaps we’ll have some rain tomorrow.’ Yet it isn’t because there is any question of drought or famine or failure of the crops. It is just for something to say.

I am trying to learn to say, ‘Good morning! Hello! It’s a lovely day today, isn’t it? Thank you very much,’ and then I will sound *really* English.

I tried it out the other day in a shop and I thought the shop man looked a bit surprised. When I went out of the shop I saw it was pouring with rain! So I had got it wrong! It *is* difficult.

Young people in England are very different from their Vietnamese counterparts. In Vietnam, families take decisions together. I have described the day in 1978 when our family made the important decision to leave our homeland. All of us were involved . . . young and old. Our father asked each of us if we wanted to leave. This is why, in Hong Kong, I was very sad when the family decided to move off to Canada without me. It was a decision for all the family. Though my mother might feel sad about leaving me behind, the decision was that the family was to go to Canada and that was that!

It is very different in England. There is a different kind of freedom. The young people make their own decisions, even when they are so young that they have little sense. And what they decide to do is often foolish.

We were more of a community. It was not just our extended families; we gained strength from the whole community. Everyone was interested in a birth or marriage or if we had important news. We always shared with our neighbours as well as our families, and our homes were freely open to each other. English people are very friendly, but they do not walk into each other's homes in the same way. They will ask permission or knock, or phone to see if it is convenient.

I was talking to Julie about this. 'We live our lives more in public,' I told her. 'We don't have a dividing line between our homes and the street. There is more space in the street for all the things we have to do. Even the dentists work in the streets, or they used to before the Communists took over, and there is massaging and card-playing going on all the time. There is real life in Vietnam streets.'

'Our streets are busy too,' Julie said, 'but perhaps we use our homes more. It's too cold for most of the year to sit out on the pavements. They're not very comfortable anyway!'

'But where are the fifty million people that the papers talk about?' I asked. I had begun to try to read the papers to know what was going on. 'Britain is supposed to be overcrowded. But on Sundays, when I walk to church, the streets are empty. Sometimes I don't see one person. Where are they all?'

Hong Kong was overcrowded. We could see it was. People were everywhere, almost falling over each other. But here there seemed to be so much space.

'When it is evening the people disappear behind their doors,' I went on. 'You never see groups of people chatting together.'

'No, you have got it all wrong,' said Julie. 'People do go out in groups. They visit the pubs; they go to clubs and discos, the cinemas and theatres and quite a number do still go to church. If you went to the pubs and discos you'd find them full all right, and thousands go to football matches.'

'I'd rather see the churches full,' I said. But I was glad to learn from Julie. After all, she is an Englishwoman, and really knows England, but I am just talking from my own observations.

One evening, a few weeks ago, I went out to buy a cassette for my recorder and all the shops were shut. It was only six o'clock and it was not dark or cold. In Vietnam the shops don't close at all. You can go out and buy something for breakfast at five o'clock and for supper at eleven! So I was very glad the other day to find there was a new kind of shop that you could use any time. I read about it in the newspaper. There were no assistants. You did everything for yourself.

Because Julie liked to help me with my English, I told her about it. I was surprised that she had not told me. Perhaps she didn't know there was such a shop!

'I've been learning about the shop with no people,' I said.

'What *do* you mean?' Julie asked.

'It says here in this paper. There are shops with no sales assistants. I expect you have to put the money in slots. It must be like in the Car Parks. You do it all yourself.'

I knew I was right this time. I had seen it in a magazine as well. It was called a 'Do It Yourself' shop. I thought it was a good idea, when the shops were closed so often. But Julie laughed and laughed. She said it didn't mean that at all. There were people in those shops, but you took the goods home and worked on them yourself. The 'do it yourself' part refers to what you do at home, not in the shop! You take a pack of wood or slots or brackets and then you put up shelves at home. I laughed too. It was funny, but I do get a little worried. I have been here for two whole years and I have only just discovered about DIY. There must be so much more that I don't know! It is quite a struggle.

One day I asked Julie the meaning of the word 'Ng'ong'. (That is how it sounded to me. I thought it was quite Chinese!) Julie was very puzzled for a long time then as I *said* it to her, she laughed.

'I've got it!' she called out, 'it's hang on!'

'That's right,' I replied, 'that's what I said. 'Ng'ong! Whatever does it mean? I can't find it in my dictionary.'

'You won't,' replied Julie. 'It's not in any dictionary at all. It's slang. It means 'Hold on! Wait a minute! Who did you hear saying it?'

'It was the electrician who came to mend the fuse. But he didn't mean me to hold on to the wires. He was talking to himself, I think.'

Since that day, I've heard many people say it. The residents here at Bethany House say it too. I have started to say it now, but they always laugh when I talk their slang. Once or twice Julie has stopped me from saying some slang words. She says it is not nice for me to say these words. It is something that a Christian would not say.

This is very worrying because I can't know whether a slang word is nice or not. So I just pray to my Lord and ask Him to keep me clean in my speaking. I like the psalm that says we can only approach God when we have clean hands and a pure heart. I think if my heart is pure, my mouth will be pure too.

I try hard not to criticise things I don't understand. We had good practice in this under the Communists in Vietnam and while I was in China. We did not criticise then because we were afraid of the consequences. I am not afraid now in the same way, but I *am* afraid to do anything to displease my Lord.

The postal service brings me many surprises . . . some good, some disappointing. Letters seem to arrive just when I need them. The English people criticise the service for being so slow, but I think it is wonderful to see the British postmen trudging through all weathers to bring us our letters. They never seem cross. It is clever the way they never muddle up the letters, especially when some are so badly addressed. In Sopley we were taught very scrupulously about how to address envelopes correctly. I am sure I do this perfectly! Teacher Frida was terribly strict about this and about filling in forms properly. I remember when I was still living in Sopley, one of my friends received a letter addressed like this:

SOHLEY Nceblon
centNe nN BNansgoNe
ThNistehusehu
DONset England.

'England' was the only correct word. The long word beginning with 'Th' was meant to be 'Christchurch'! How did the postman know?! That letter came all the way from Hong-Kong.

I had letters from my family newly resettled in Canada and from Xuan Linh in Tientsin in China. I have also heard two or three times from Noelle. The last letter I had from her told of her coming marriage. I certainly hope she will be happy; she began my happiness for me and I will never forget her.

Some letters have been very hard to take and I have found them difficult to accept as part of God's plan for my life. When the Canadian authorities finally wrote, saying it was impossible for me to live in Canada, and I realised I might never see my family again, I was very upset. I know the verse in Romans 8 that says that all things work together for good, but I was sure that it would be best for me to go to Canada and tell the Good News of Jesus to my family. I had not really learnt to *trust* God in all my circumstances. Sometimes I still think I know better than my Lord, even though I know that is a dreadful thing to admit.

I find it a hard struggle to gain spiritual maturity. When I had been in Southampton for a short time, I felt it was right for me to be baptised. Because I had been helped so much at Hurn Church, I wanted to be baptised there. I knew very little then, but I wanted to tell people that I believed that Jesus had saved me from my sins and from myself. It was a wonderful day in my life. I was glad to give my testimony and I felt I was very spiritual and mature at that time, but now I look back, I see how very simple and immature my understand was. I was like the man in Mark 8, who had his eyes opened by Jesus, but at first could only see men as trees walking about! Nothing was really clear. Now I do understand a little more; when we are Christians we need to be separated from the world. Now I understand that when I was baptised, it was a symbol of dying with Jesus, and when I came into new life, I knew I had nothing to do with this world.

I look back and see all the different people who have been instruments in my spiritual life . . . all very necessary to my growth! There was Noelle right at the beginning; then later, as I learnt from the Bible at Hurn Church, I began to see the light more clearly; later still, after my baptism, I was challenged at the Chinese Church to grow further. All these people were teaching me in the way I needed at the time in order to grow.

At first I was like the Corinthians; I was not ready for the solid food, and as St Paul fed them on 'milk', so my teachers fed me with simple, pure spiritual food. Then as I grew in my spiritual life, I was able to take a little solid food. Sometimes it was hard to take, because it made me realise how full of failings I was.

Now I am a member of the Chinese Church and am able to remember my Lord Jesus every Sunday in the breaking of bread. This is a very great privilege, but it is also a responsibility. I must walk in a worthy way as a Christian. I am given excellent teaching by the Chinese leaders and I have time for a great deal of Bible Study, but I am still aware how far short I fall; just as my right leg drags behind me as I walk, so I lag behind my brothers and sisters in the faith.

Looking back over my life, I can see lessons in all the things that happened to me. I even remember my solemn thoughts as I stood on the Great Wall of China way back in 1966. *Then* I thought about the Wall with patriotic pride, for 'I am always a Chinese man' (as the poet Lang Youwei wrote), but now I began to see a new significance. Those ancient men gave their lives to save future generations from the wild barbarians. This was splendid, but they did not sacrifice willingly. It was forced labour. Our Lord Jesus gave His life for all the world, but His sacrifice was a willing one. He gave His life as a ransom for all. I thought too of God the Father willingly offering His only son Jesus for the sins of the world, so that we all might have true freedom.

I thought about the loss of my wife and child, and then, later, the separation from my family, and realised that I had to feel utter loneliness and rejection before I could experience the wealth of God's love and acceptance.

I could see a more practical lesson in the fact that I had to learn to speak the English language before I could live confidently in this country. And, because I had always been good at language learning, this was quite a blow to my pride. I did not . . . in fact, I *do* not . . . find it easy at all. But the desperate attempts to learn and my reliance on God have brought forth some success.

I think back to the Gate of Heavenly Peace, and I see that there is no peace on earth apart from the God of Peace. Seeing those crowds of wild Red Guards milling about in that square, wrecking ancient relics of Chinese culture and destroying the beautiful things, was totally opposed to the peace that Jesus spoke of to His disciples. 'Peace I leave with you; *My* peace I give to you, not as the world gives . . .' Yet still, to me, that Gate of

Heavenly Peace was like a poor incomplete symbol of the real Gate, the Door through which I have entered and found his Peace.

Sometimes I think back to the terrible month we spent on the wild seas, and because of that dreadful time, I know better than many people the meaning of the beautiful English hymn:

Jesu, Lover of my soul
Let me to Thy bosom fly,
While the nearer waters roll,
While the tempest still is high:
Hide me, O my Saviour, hide,
Till the storm of life is past;
Safe into the haven guide;
O receive my soul at last!

Hong Kong may have been our haven at that time, and we were so grateful for it, but the real haven is Jesus Himself and there is no other refuge.

One of my favourite psalms is Psalm 46, which begins with the words: 'God is our refuge and strength, a very present help in trouble. Therefore we will not fear though the earth should change, though the mountains shake in the heart of the sea; though its waters roar and foam; though the mountains tremble with its tumult.' This psalm even sounds good in the English language!

I look back to the long time I had to spend in the hospital in Southampton. I have forgotten the suffering now, but I realise that it was there that I came to know Lo and, through him, all the others at the Chinese Church who have since become my friends.

After a time in Southampton, I began to feel secure. I was well; my heart did not trouble me at all. I had plenty of energy. But one night I awoke, feeling very ill indeed, so ill, in fact, that I had a job to crawl along to Julie's room. There was no need to tell her I was ill. She phoned immediately for the doctor and, in a very short time, the ambulance arrived to take me to the hospital. I had thought I had finished with hospitals!

Apparently I had had a rupture in my left groin for some time. The hospital knew about this in Hong Kong, but it was only now that it had become a serious condition. If the hospital had not managed to catch it in time, I might easily have had a strangulated hernia. As it was, they were able to treat me with fluids to keep me from becoming dehydrated and to rest my bowels. After a month I returned home again, and later, I had successful repair surgery.

I think there was a lesson in this for me too. The Lord was teaching me I had no security at all apart from Him. I had to rely *entirely* on Him. My strength was only in Him.

In Vietnam, as a young man, I was very strong physically; then followed my long years of illness, and I became physically weak. Then came my knowledge of Jesus Christ as my Saviour. He lifted me up and held my right hand and guided me all my days. I had to be made weak before I could enjoy God's strength. Then my strength was all in Him. 'When I am weak, then I am strong' (2.Cor.12:10).

So, I am still in school, learning all the time. My *life* is like a school. I have to work hard at my English; I have to learn to adjust to the Western culture and to my life in the small community at Bethany House, and most important of all, I must learn from the Lord. He did not only say, 'Follow Me!' and 'Come unto Me!' He said, 'Learn from Me!' and He is the best teacher anyone could have.

CONCLUSION

A Visit To Sang. Hope for the future

Once again Sang was entertaining me in his home in Bethany House. We had been talking over the past, and I had been looking at the photos of his family.

'Have you any other mementoes of your escape from Vietnam?' I asked him.

'You're sitting on one of them,' he laughed.

'This?' I enquired with surprise, pointing to his bedcover. It looked so very English: a blue folk-weave bedspread. 'How is this a memento?' Perhaps he hadn't understood the word, though his English was improving in leaps and bounds. His perseverence was certainly paying off.

Sang laughed loudly as he nodded his head. 'This was my only cover on the boat,' he said, 'it saw me through the typhoon and all my time in Hong Kong . . . and . . .' he reached into a drawer, 'here's another souvenir.'

He brought out a half-broken black comb that did look a little the worse for wear. 'I still use it,' he said.

'But I have a better reminder than these things,' he went on. 'My little Chinese New Testament that Noelle gave to me helps me remember how God had a plan for my life right through. That is something I want to remember. I would like to forget the bad things. The Bible, God's Word, is the link between the old life and the new. This takes me on into the future.'

'What hopes have you for the future?' I asked Sang.

His face lit up. 'I am hoping that the Lord will allow me to visit my family in Canada,' he said. 'The Canadian authorities will not permit me to live there. I can't think why they are so against having me, when my family are all there. They would look after me and I am well now.'

'Do you think you could do a job?' I asked him rather hesitantly. His life had been so filled with illness and operations, and his right arm was still useless. But his answer was confident.

'Oh yes. I could interpret. There are many Vietnamese people there who need a translator, or I could work on the Bible. I would like to translate the Christian testimonies of people so that Vietnamese friends could read them and learn to trust the Lord. There are so many broken, useless lives as mine was, and they can be mended.'

'Do you have any other ambitions?' I asked. 'Any other reasons for wanting to go to Canada?'

'I want most of all,' he answered, 'to share the Good News of Jesus Christ with all my family . . . with my father and mother before it is too late . . . with Hung and Thanh and Thuy and all my little nieces and nephews. I feel as if I have a surplus of joy in me. It wants to overflow to everyone. It is sad that everyone doesn't want to listen. In London, none of my friends want to listen.'

'Why do you think this is?' I asked him, for I had wondered about it too. There had been no hesitation at all with Sang. As he said himself, he went to Noelle's Bible Study just to listen, though he did not believe. 'He listened and he believed.' It was as simple as that.

'The reason is that the Vietnamese have been deeply influenced by the atheists. The books that were used in the schools and colleges were all anti-Christian. They taught atheistic evolution.'

'Was there no freedom of choice at all?'

'No, none,' Sang replied. 'I didn't realise then, but there was no spiritual freedom at all. It did not worry me because I was an atheist myself. Looking back, I can see that the Communists used false reason to destroy those who had any faith at all. They were against all religions but most of all against Christianity. So now, when I talk with my friends in London or other places, they are polite and they do listen but they do not really hear. They may hear with their ears, but they have shut up their hearts to God's Holy Spirit.'

'How do you think it came about that *you* listened and *heard*?' I enquired. Again the radiant smile flashed across his face.

'I believe that the Lord had been preparing me for some time. Even in my early years, when I was so carefree, I felt there was something extra that had not yet entered my life . . . when I was so ill and my life was despaired of, still I came through. There must be something, I thought. Later I felt it was not some*thing* but Some*one*! In a way, I was ready for the missionaries and their message. God's plan for my life had begun.'

'And do you think you have discovered the whole of God's plan yet?' I began, but with a laugh, Sang stopped me.

'Of course not!' Sang was obviously amused at the question. 'My Christian life is only just beginning. It is so exciting; I can't wait to see what is round the next corner. I feel as if I am in training for something . . . but I don't know what!'

'Does it worry you? Are you anxious?'

'No . . . How can I be? You're not anxious, are you, Teacher Frida?'

I was silent. With so many things to cause him anxiety, with so many uncertainties, how could *I* admit to moments of worry? My life had been like a smooth passage on a summer's day compared with Sang's turbulent voyage. But he was so honest. I had to be truthful too. 'Yes, Sang,' I replied. The pause had been a long one. Perhaps he sensed the tension before my answers.

'Sometimes I am anxious, but I should not be. Like you, I am still learning. I know that when I cast all my cares upon the Lord, He cares for me and like you, I know who holds the future. One of my biggest hopes is that I will trust the Lord utterly and entirely. What would you say is *your* greatest hope?' I continued, though in a way he had told me already.

'I have two greatest hopes and they're tied up with each other.' He smiled though he spoke with deep feeling. 'I hope with great earnestness to see my family again soon . . . and . . . ' (He picked up his Bible that was never far away, and read from Hebrews 11), 'I am longing for a better country. This Scripture speaks of aliens and strangers on earth. That is what I am now, and my family too. Though I have found a good home in England, I am still a foreigner, (this with a beam of joy holding no bitterness) but in the better country, the heavenly one, I will not be a stranger at all. God has prepared me a place to live . . . better than England . . . better than Canada . . . better than Vietnam . . . a real home for ever.'

'Like the heavenly mansion in John 14?' I enquired.

'Yes, just like that,' Sang answered readily. 'That is my favourite chapter in the whole Bible. *That* is why my heart is not troubled. Jesus said, 'Let not your heart be troubled, nor let it be afraid!'

As I listened to this still-new Christian, who had been through so much suffering, I felt a wonderful sense of peace within my heart. Here was Sang, comforting me with the words of Jesus that had comforted him. What a family is the family of God! We suffer together. We rejoice together.

But this line of thinking brought me back to Sang and his earthly family, far away in Canada.

'So . . . these are your two greatest hopes? To see your family and to be with the Lord and His family?'

'Yes, but more than that,' he went on. 'Those are two separate things and I pray for both, but most of all I hope that all my family will learn to love Jesus my Lord as I have done, so that we may *all* go to a better country

. . . a heavenly one. God has saved me and made me one of His family. He loves them too; Jesus died for them all. Why should He not have them too? I have great hope for that.'

And looking at Sang and knowing the strength and continuity of his prayer for his family, I have hope too.

> 'We rejoice in our hope of sharing the glory of God. More than that, we rejoice in our sufferings, knowing that suffering produces endurance, and endurance produces character, and character produces hope, and hope does not disappoint us, because God's love has been poured into our hearts through the Holy Spirit, which has been given to us.'
>
> (Romans 5:1-5.)

POSTSCRIPT

What has happened to the refugees? Where are they all? Are they settled? Have any of them jobs? Are they happy?

These are just some of the many questions that are still being asked around the country. The massive exodus of 1979-81 may be over, the reception centres are closed, the organisation of teachers of English to the refugees (adults and children) has been disbanded, but the interest continues, as shown in this type of enquiry.

There are more personal questions too. 'What happened to that lovely little family that came to our social, our church . . . our Christmas party? . . . Do you ever see that lonely young man who had a speech defect? . . . Did that wonderful seamstress get a job? . . . Where has that man who had open-heart surgery gone? Is he well? . . . Do you keep up with them all?'

The last question is easy to answer. No, it is impossible to keep up with all the refugees that pass through one's hands. Mercifully, hearts are large enough to cherish memories and real friendships, even if the refugees have found their way to Wales, Scotland or the USA. Letters follow their departure and must, of course, be answered, but generally members of support groups become friends and take over where teachers and staff leave off. Superficial distant caring is not sufficient for people who are struggling to cope with social isolation, the British way of life and the language problem. They need a family or an individual with time and affection to offer.

Sadly, many of our own people discuss the refugee

problem from afar or from the security and comfort of an armchair. There is still ignorance, but the British Refugee Council is only too willing to supply information. For the genuinely concerned, there are facts and figures available and places of resettlement and numbers of families will be provided on request.

All the refugees have been settled somewhere and if they have not been allocated to the place of their choice, in *that* they share common ground with many of the British people, who are searching for homes and jobs. Almost all the refugees place London as their first choice, with other large cities taking a second or third place. The name of London still spells glamour for many (as had Hong Kong), the city of many refugees, the place of Chinese restaurants and potential jobs! Even as the British teenager has to come to terms with the real London, so do the refugees!

Life has not been easy for the 16,000 Vietnamese refugees who are now resettled in Britain. Many of them are unskilled and, like Sang, were turned down by Canada or the USA, who were more selective than Britain. There is an extremely high rate of unemployment among them. As we have seen, even an able linguist like Sang had great difficulties learning English, and in fact only 20 per cent of the refugees are now really proficient in the language. The problems and stresses have sometimes led to depression and marital breakdowns, though many of the refugees are happy and have settled well.

There is another question that we should ask ourselves. Have the Vietnamese and other refugees *taken* only from Britain? How about the richness of their experience, which if we are willing to learn and be sensitive to it, may be taken by us and incorporated into our heritage?

A breadth of vision entered our lives when the refugees entered our country; a depth of sharing their sorrows and suffering extended our sympathies. With their grace, their gratitude and their indomitable grit, they have worked their gentle way into our land, our homes, our lives. And we can use their gifts or exploit them! We can add their gifts to ours and increase the richness of gratitude, grace and grit that we ourselves need.

Theirs is the gratitude that always needs to repay simple kindnesses; 'We give to you, dear my teacher,' they say or write. 'You so kind.'

Theirs is the grace with which they speak and act. Even the way they shake hands or hand you a bag is like a caress.

Theirs is the grit with which they met and bore and overcame their immense difficulties and hardships and set to work to learn our language.

NB: The Vietnamese refugees have much to give us and teach us, but they need our friendship too.

For details about Vietnamese, and other refugees, write to:

British Refugee Council
36, Westminster Palace Gardens
Artillery Row
LONDON SW1P 1RR

Since writing this story, Sang has had one of his hopes realised. After months of frustration he has passed his medical examination, obtained his visa and left for Canada on August 1st, 1984.

What a reunion in Toronto in the new Chinese home with Sang's parents and almost forty of his 'extended' family!

We await further news that the second of his heart's desires has been granted too. Sang has enough hope for that also.